Some people only talk about advancing women of colour into leadership; others consider it or join a committee to make it happen. But Winitha lives it and makes it happen for women all over the world, inspiring us all.

Yamini Naidu
The world's only economist turned storyteller

#ColourFULL explores many of the challenges that women of colour face and equips as well as encourages women of colour and their allies. Winitha Bonney's passion and empathy are captured in this book, as is her steadfast commitment to advancing the individual and collective success of women of colour. Winitha is a contemporary thought leader, positive role model and powerful advocate.

Rachel Tulia
Executive Director Corporate Delivery Services
Victorian Public Service

Winitha is a thought leader and change maker - this book is written from her personal experience in way women of colour can relate - she makes us feel we are not alone in the challenges that we face - she makes us feel like we are understood and that she's got your back! This unique book will give you practical tools and tips for women of colour from a woman of colour - to feel confident and able to operate from a place of personal power and abundance - through her words and experience, she will encourage you to reclaim your power and amplify it and go on to change the world!

Malini Raj
Cultural Diversity and Inclusion Advocate

Through personal stories, wit, and candour Winitha shares her experiences as a woman of colour navigating spaces where it is not uncommon to be the lonely 'only'. #ColourFULL serves up a warm embrace packed with necessary truths, insightful affirmations, encouragement and actionable advice for women around the world going through similar experiences to push through and overcome.

Dr Cortina McCurry
CEO, Caia

Winitha is a fierce voice of this generation. #ColourFull is an uplifting, inspiring and refreshing account of what it feels like to be 'the other' or the only one in the room. It is an incredibly lonely journey – but this book makes you feel like you're not alone and that you can truly take over the world. I feel proud of my colour, and this book will make you honour your heritage too! A recommended read for all WoC who are determined to succeed in life unapologetically.

Cathy Ngo
Keynote Speaker, Writer and Founder, Keynoteworthy

#Colour FULL

How Women of Colour can become powerful
leaders that transform the world

WINITHA BONNEY OAM

First published in 2021 by Hambone Publishing
Melbourne, Australia
Book design and layout: Sadie Butterworth-Jones and Russell Caras
Editing: Elizabeth Carr
Cover photography: Molly Burmeister | @mollyburmeisterphotography

For information about this title, contact:
Winitha Bonney
hello@winitha.com | www.winitha.com

ISBN 978-1-922357-24-3 (paperback)
ISBN 978-1-922357-25-0 (ebook)

Dedication

To God, who called me to do this work and continues to prosper me.

To my mum and dad, whose hard work laid the foundation and opportunity for my success and who are incredible grandparents to our little potato.

To my guardian angel Bubbles, writing companion, hot water bottle and best friend.

To Kemi, who first saw and heard me. You show me every day what's possible. And my team, mentors and allies who continue to support me.

And lastly to you, wonderful warrior Woman of Colour. May this book bless and transform you so that you may transform others and the world. From my heart to yours, may you be free.

Contents

Acknowledgement of country

I want to acknowledge the traditional land on which you and I stand on today. This incredible land that we have the opportunity to work, live and play on. I want to give my deepest respect to any First Nations people reading this book and to their elders past, present and future. I want to acknowledge and honour their strength, resilience, wisdom, love and generosity as well as their incredible power, culture, community and connection to land. Sovereignty was never ceded. This land always was, always will be Aboriginal land.

If you identify as a non–Indigenous Women of Colour, we have a responsibility to get 100% behind our First Nations colleagues, friends and community to stand by them in unwavering solidarity and love and be their biggest allies and cheerleaders. Allyship is not an option, it's an obligation and expectation. It's not about saving, it's about serving. It's not about your saying you support First Nations people it's about taking action and getting stuck into the doing, day in, day out. May we continue to serve and elevate First Nations people in Australia and around the world.

Who this book is for

Although this book uses the terms 'women' and 'Women of Colour,' they are used in an inclusive sense. It is for those who self–identify as a Woman of Colour and actively includes those that have been affected by misogyny similar to women (meaning cis and non–binary, transgender, gender non–conforming and genderqueer). However you identify, may you get what you need here and what your heart and soul desires.

Who is a Woman of Colour?

"There had been so many times in my life when I'd found myself the only Woman of Colour – or even the only woman, period – sitting at a conference table or attending a board meeting or mingling at one VIP gathering or another. If I was the first at some of these things, I wanted to make sure that in the end I wasn't the only – that others were coming up behind me. "

~ Michelle Obama, Becoming

In her book, Becoming, Michelle Obama speaks to the experiences of many Women of Colour in terms of identity, opportunity and inequality. As someone who specialises in closing the gap for Women of Colour in leadership and entrepreneurship, there are times when I am asked, 'Who is a Woman of Colour?' I have never seen myself as a multicultural or culturally and linguistically diverse woman. I see myself as a Woman of Colour. Perhaps it is because for a period of time I lived and worked in Canada and the United States where the term is more widely used. For me, the term is powerful because we created it for ourselves. Regardless of where the term originated, it is a term of power, not a label put on us by a government, system or institution.

It's important that we know the history to understand the term's true meaning. 'Woman of Colour' was first used at the 1977 National Women's Conference in Houston, Texas. At this conference, a group of trailblazing African American women formed the Black Women's Agenda and carried with them into the conference a Black Women's Plan of Action to replace a measly three pages that had been embedded into the 200-page conference report and given the title 'Minority Women's Plank report' and given the title 'Minority Women's Plank report'. Not only did they bring their own report into the conference, but these pioneering Black women also renamed it to reclaim power from the condescension of the term 'minority.' When other 'minority' women heard this, they also wanted to be included in the agenda and negotiations to rename the group led to the term 'Women of Colour.' Activist Loretta Ross said about the conference, 'They didn't see it as a biological designation – you're born Asian, you're born Black, you're born African American, whatever – but it is a solidarity definition, a commitment to work in collaboration with other oppressed Women of Colour who have been 'minoritised.' This is a term that has a lot of power for us.' From the outset, this term has been used politically and socially in the context of all women who experience systemic racism with relationship to the varied

Western and European cultures. Importantly, a Woman of Colour is one who self–identifies as such and unlike the term suggests, is not reflective of the colour of her skin. Fundamentally, the term unites those who experience oppression, suppression, systemic racism, inequity and inequality.

> *Being called a Woman of Colour is powerful to me. It is about taking back power of the term 'colour' and redefining the narrative around it for yourself and your sisters.*
>
> **#ColourFULL**

The term 'Woman of Colour' also brings together two layers that create complexity to our lives as well as acknowledging the host of gender and cultural diversity barriers and challenges that we experience in advancing in our careers and lives. It narrows and defines the focus and is inclusive of those that also identify as non–binary, transgender, gender non–conforming and genderqueer.

I was told from a young age that dark skin was not beautiful. Growing up, my aunties would tell me, 'Yuck, you're black.' I can go as far as to say that people with dark skin have been feared purely on the basis of the amount of melanin in their skin. Period. Our Indigenous and African sisters have also been referred to as 'coloured' while experiencing extreme acts of racism. Some of us have in our bathroom cupboards the toxic lightening creams and serums that are sold in our local ethnic grocery stores. You might have even seen some of our aunties walking around in summer holding an umbrella. Such is the relationship to the colour of skin. On the flip side, I have African sisters from a spectrum of melanin skin tones who don't want to be labelled as a Black woman or Woman of Colour but simply as a woman, others that only define themselves only as a Black woman, some who define themselves only as an African woman and some that define themselves as a Black African woman and a Woman of Colour. I also have Indigenous sisters who define themselves as First Nations and a Woman of Colour and some that identify only as a Blak and First Nations woman. It can be argued that words such as Black and White and even the concept of race are political and social constructs used a form oppression and suppression and part of systemic, structural and institutional discrimination. To others it is a form of empowerment and identity. The above is a reflection of these differences.

> *Being a Woman of Colour comes down to self–identity. It is not about labelling various ethnicities or skin tones. It is about uniting those who experience systemic racism and oppression so that collectively we can all advance.*
>
> ***#ColourFULL***

My work is around supporting those who define themselves as a Woman of Colour and have experienced systemic racism and oppression to ignite themselves and those around them to be changemakers, supporting the work to close the inequality and inequity gap for Women of Colour. Until we reach justice and equity, my work is not done. There is power in words and defining the experiences of gender and culture barriers so that we can have the necessary conversations and take the action we need to take.

Introduction

"As women of colour, we are among a generation accomplishing firsts – whether the first in our families to attend college, enter a traditional workplace, or embark on a nontraditional path.
Just as we are often firsts, it's not unusual for us also to be "onlies": the only woman in the room; the only person of colour; and the only one bringing our particular set of experiences to our workplaces, classrooms and teams.
...[hear] a different voice – your own, strong voice – and [remind yourself] that what you bring into any room is valuable.
No matter what your profession, vocation or field of endeavour, if you are a woman looking to blaze your own trail and forge your own firsts, and if you are wondering whether your life and experiences matter, or whether what you bring with you as you begin your journey is enough, you are not alone.."

—Cecilia Muñoz, *More Than Ready*

A confession

For many years my favourite place to live had been in self–pity. In the early years, I spent a lot of time feeling sorry for myself and whingeing to anyone that would give me airtime, but I learned the hard way that this doesn't bring personal power, growth, success or results. Expecting everyone else and everything to change just so I could survive let alone thrive only led to psychological and soul trauma; the damaging of my mental health, spirit, potential and inner personal power. That said, there are many things in life that we as Women of Colour can't change. We can't change the trauma in our lives or that within our community, ancestors, culture or that of those we love or the sad fact that it happened. We can't change the generational effects of slavery and colonisation or that it occurred. It's not our responsibility to dismantle and decolonise systemic discrimination and racism. We can, however, thrive despite structural oppression by getting equipped with tools and strategies to not only revolt against it but to collectively create a revolution by campaigning for our collective and individual success and equitable freedom. In the process, we empower, elevate and possibly free our sisters, community and future generations.

\#

A revolution empowers us to revolt from a place of personal power by pushing through internalised suppression and past external barriers and challenges.

#ColourFULL

Advocacy is a necessary and extremely important piece to freedom, equity and equality for Women of Colour but it is evident that it alone is not enough to achieve full systemic change and therefore success in our lives. If it was, we'd be seeing more Women of Colour leaders and entrepreneurs sitting in equitable positions of power and influence creating impact. What I've seen instead is more liberation for White women and hardly any for Women of Colour. We call this White feminism. More on this later in the book. What keeps us stuck, stagnant and powerless is when we try to live from a place of negative emotions: hurt, pain, anger, resentment; fear and limiting beliefs. That's exactly the dangerous place the oppressor wants us to stay in. As Women of Colour, we need to spend less time in the negative trauma space inflicted by systemic suppression, oppression and discrimination. When we choose to stay in that place, we only deepen our wounds and trauma, causing us to be even more frustrated and powerless. Again, exactly where the oppressor wants you to be: powerless. It's the same with your career. If you haven't taken action to heal from past trauma and pain, then you're only going to sink deeper into that pain and trauma and remain powerless. These emotions are real and true, of course, it's important to name our emotions, feel and walk through them and take the time to soothe and heal but sitting in them for a lifetime does not lead us to healing and therefore success, freedom and leadership. As you will read in this book or already know from my work, I always say that the first step to becoming a leader as a Woman of Colour is in healing.

I'm big on Women of Colour knowing how brilliant we are and operating from a place of personal power and abundance. I believe that change happens when stuff changes. And in order for stuff to change, well, it takes people; it's pretty simple, isn't it? I simply refuse to believe that my power, career and life are in the hands of others. Instead, I've reclaimed my life and power by healing and empowering myself and all the Women of Colour around the world that I impact and reach every day. In the process, by focusing on what is within my ability to change, control or influence, I have rewritten my outer world and created success that is meaningful for me while creating true freedom for myself and others.

We do not live in a denial or ignorance of White and masculine systems and oppressors, pretending that these things do not affect us or that they exist. We do however, spend time thinking why they exist and how they operate in order to strategise; to stay two steps ahead, manage and navigate around, over, under and through them to succeed and thrive. We do this from a place of personal power, not powerlessness which only leads to internalised suppression, again exactly where the oppressor wants you to be. This is the key. Look to what you can control. Take action to self–preserve and amplify your personal power and radiance. When you do, you create a revolution – freeing your soul and transforming the world in the process.

> *Power is in the execution of knowledge, not in the knowledge itself.*
>
> ***#ColourFULL***

Having the courage to change the things that are in our control and acknowledging that we have the power to dictate the course of our own life will get us moving, growing, learning, achieving and turn our deepest desires and dreams into reality.

We can reclaim our power and amplify it if we choose to: pay less attention to the negative chatter that is going around in your mind and instead decide to take 100% responsibility for the things that you can control, change or influence in your life, internally and externally.

Who can use this book

We are an ambitious lot who are frustrated yet have a deep desire to be the leaders we know we truly are inside. We know that we deserve to fulfil our potential and step into leadership. We know what's not working and what our internal and external barriers are but we are struggling because we don't have the practical and proven tools and tactics to achieve true freedom, peace, success, abundance, wealth, joy or fulfilment.

Women of Colour need an awakening and need answers. A way forward, up and out: a revolution. We are ready to rise, we are empowered Women of Colour warriors and leaders and we are about to start something big: a revolution that will free ourselves by driving us forward and into healing. From healing we can then be empowered to take consistent powerful, deeply intentional and focused action to begin to create success and freedom in our career, business and life. This book is the revolution you have been looking for. A refusal to fall victim. A call to arms as a community and the equipping of 'armoury' and 'inner weapons' that will support your quest to weaken and conquer structural discrimination and racism for freedom in the systemic and spiritual war against the oppressors. Will you join us?

If you are to be victorious and not victimised, it is up to you to take the first step. The first step towards reclaiming your life and future is an internal one and it starts with acceptance and surrender and ends in courage and wisdom. The serenity prayer says, 'God grant me the serenity to accept the things I cannot change, the courage to change the things I can and the wisdom to know the difference.' When we choose to put the serenity prayer into practice, take 100% responsibility for the things that are in our control and have the courage and wisdom to change them; and accept and let go of the things we can't, that's when we render ourselves from victim to victorious, from powerless to powerful and in the process reclaim, leverage and amplify our identity, potential and personal power. The next step is to rewrite the foundation on which you create success – that's an external job. Far too often we jump straight to part two, attempting to rewrite our outer external world through a job promotion, postgraduate degree or leadership opportunity. This is why we are perpetually struggling and stagnant. Sustainable long–term success and leadership that truly impacts, influences and transforms the world is an internal job. It starts with part one. 80% of your success comes from the work you do in your internal world.

This book is for Women of Colour who are frustrated with where they currently are. Those who do not wish to live life as a powerless victim and who refuse to wait any longer for equality to happen and are ready instead to, as the first African American congresswoman, Shirley Chisholm said, 'Bring your own folding chair' to the table.

In this book, we are going to help you become the leader you always knew you were deep down, create success on your terms and get a seat at the table.

This book will:

\#   Give you practical steps and a roadmap to reclaim your personal power, confidence and conviction to get unstuck and be the warrior leader you always knew you were.

\#   Take you on a deep dive into your inner world and give you practical actions to build a solid foundation for a sustainable and successful long–term leadership career.

\#   Equip you with the tools and strategies to revolt against, overcome and conquer systemic oppression by rewriting your outer world so that you can thrive in White structures.

\#   Teach you how to powerfully increase your visibility through proven tactics to take your leadership and career revolution to the next level.

\#   Build, cultivate and strengthen your leadership skills from the inside out to create global impact and influence.

\#   Halve the time it takes for you to achieve your goals and create success on your terms.

This book is based on my years of research and thought leadership into advancing Women and People of Colour, as well as the hundreds of hours I have spent in deep, intentional, interviews, group–based conversations and one–on–one coaching and mentoring conversations with Women of Colour from around the world. This book is also based on my lived experience, how I've leveraged and navigated masculine and White systems to succeed on my terms and what I've learned in my career over the last 22+ years.

A call to arms and action!

What I want to give to people like you and me are the tools to revolt against and tear down systemic oppressors. Change is made by people like us who are sick and tired and who create a revolution. Women of Colour who tear down the walls and over take the city with wit, strategy and pure cleverness like in the story of the Trojan horse. For us, over taking the city is attaining success on our terms and achieving leadership positions of impact and influence despite systemic discrimination and racism (the walls and gates of the city).

Even the poorest and those who have suffered greatly have the power to create change in their world. There are countless stories etched in our past and current history of Women of Colour leaders who have overcome insurmountable hurdles, fathomless trauma and challenges to create success and freedom. What is so inspiring in these stories is that in creating change these same people have given permission for others to do the same; paving the way forward, creating a powerful blueprint and shining a light on the path. We couldn't have come this far if it were not for those brave, bold and courageous few who refused to be a victim and instead viewed themselves as powerful.

I believe in you and your incredible potential to create your own reality and a life you feel proud of. There is no fear in going after what you want and there is nothing to lose. Instead, there is everything to gain. There is only fear in staying where you are for the next 20 years wondering what could have been and living a life of crippling regret. Go after what you want, step outside your comfort zone and lean into the hard, difficult, challenging and vulnerable journey to reach success and leadership on the other side, I speak from experience and the countless Women of Colour leaders I've interviewed when I say 'It's worth it, Sis.' As they say, 'Do the easy things life will be hard, do the hard things and life will be easy.' I choose the hard things, to revolt and create a revolution for the sake of myself and my sisters and invite you to do so too. Collectively we are stronger.

I want to be a changemaker, someone who causes a revolution and, in the process, sets other sisters free. I want my life to be fucking amazing. I want to be powerful, exceptional, unapologetic and relentless and I want my career to be incredible. I'm absolutely positive that by picking up this book you want exactly that too.

Refuse to let your words, feelings, thoughts and behaviours position you as a disempowered and powerless Women of Colour at the mercy of oppressors. Set yourself free from the psychological shackles of modern–day slavery and reclaim your abundant and brilliant power.

#ColourFULL

Get up, get moving. Equip yourself with the right tools and strategies to revolt against systemic oppression and stand side by side in solidarity with your sisters to create a revolution collectively. You are not stuck and you are not powerless. You are not a victim. You are powerful beyond measure. You are an incredible warrior queen who will transform the world through exceptional and masterful leadership. This promise for your future is waiting for you right now. You are already the leader you so desperately want to be. You just need a space for reflection and healing, a gentle prod, some tools and someone (me) to cheer you on.

I'm just like you, trying things out, running with what works and dropping the rest; making mistakes, falling down, getting back up, getting hurt, healing and reclaiming my power, resisting, pushing and fighting back, strategising, levelling up and trying again. I'm on this journey with you, walking every step of the way with you cheering you on and loving you in the good and bad times. This book is from my heart to yours; may it bless you, transform your life and prosper you so that you can change the world. I've got your back, Sister. Let's do this together and create a revolution!

PART 1

RECLAIM YOUR INNER WORLD

1

Warrior leadership: the journey

"Women of Colour warriors are constant warriors who dig in bare earth to feed the hungry child, who pray for health the bedside of the sick when there is no medicine, who fashion a toy to make a poor child smile, who take to the streets demanding freedom, freedom, freedom against armed police. Every act of survival by a woman of colour is an act of resistance to the holocaust and the war. No soldier fights harder than a woman warrior for she fights for total change, for a new order in a world in which can finally rest and love."

~ June Jordan, Where is the Love?

Why warrior leadership?

As Women of Colour, we face additional barriers and challenges to White women, men and other non–Women of Colour. Ancestrally and culturally, we have our own definition, beliefs, approach and views about what leadership looks like, and what it is. Leadership to us isn't as the world knows it. I have been inspired by stories such as Amina of Zaria and Rani of Jhansi: warrior Women of Colour who were exceptional leaders and performed on the battlefield better than any man in their army. There are countless stories scattered in our past, the blueprint is there, all we need to do is look. This is the leadership we need to adopt to thrive. A total level–up, a transformation into something so powerful that we would become a force to be reckoned with and our efforts would truly change the world. Know that this same blood runs through your veins. You are a warrior leader, we just need to create space, energy and time to bring her to the forefront from the rubble of discrimination, trauma, internalised suppression and colonisation that has built up around you. That is what this book will help you do and why I wrote it for you. You, dear sister, deserve no less.

The warrior mindset

As Women of Colour, we need to adapt the mindset and approach of warriorship because you know that we are facing two, three or 10 times the barriers and challenges to leadership of White people and men. A study by Diversity Council Australia titled *Cracking the Glass–Cultural Ceiling*, said that women from culturally diverse backgrounds experience a 'double glass ceiling'; in the USA, research by Catalyst states that 'While White women held almost one–third (32.8%) of total management positions in the US in 2020, women of color held a much smaller share,' with Asian women at 2.2%, Black women at 4.1% and Hispanic women at 4.5% (Catalyst, *Women of Color in the United States: Quick Take,* 2021).

*We must pursue warrior leadership to self–protect,
self–preserve, self–amplify and ultimately reclaim what
is rightfully ours, our power.*

#ColourFULL

We must pursue leadership: breathing and living everyday like a warrior to overcome feeling constantly tired, frustrated and exhausted from our day–to–day efforts like we are constantly walking up an insurmountable mountain.

We need to get and stay psychologically, emotionally, intellectually and spiritually fit (inner fitness) as well as physically, socially and environmentally (outer fitness) to build stamina and endurance to continue to do the hard–yards, as well as reframe and use the tough times as training grounds to build anti–fragility and resilience to prepare us for the future. Our inner fitness must seek a meaningful balance in achieving success in our external world while pursuing that incredible success which awaits in our inner world – the 'inside job' of success.

Once we can tune into this internal intensity and ferocity, a flame and passion pumps through our body, soul and mind – a deep knowing and belief that this is what we deserve and with the right training, tools, strategy and execution of our plan we will transform the world as powerful leaders with one strategic step, one action, at a time; constantly moving forward, hearts ablaze for the young Women of Colour that follow behind us.

What warrior leadership is

By living from a place of warrior and viewing leadership from that context it immediately forces and asks us to reframe what we think leadership is and what it could be. Warrior leadership has nothing to do with violence, although the term 'warrior' may sometimes allude to this. It's about strategy, foresight, oversight, hindsight and tactics. It's about spending the time to create a plan, train for it and execute it masterfully; being agile, tactile and sharp to what's happening at the front line, the battlefield, as you charge forward towards leadership.

What we know about remarkable warriors is that what happens off the field is just as important as what happens on it; it's all in the preparation, planning and training. Warrior leaders boldly and courageously engage in intense training nuanced to their unique needs, attributes and lived experience. They spend the time to craft clever plans and execute them brilliantly. We need to create our own 'inner' gym and get 'fit' through consistent and rigorous warrior mindset training. Make a plan, stay focused and stay on your game because success is when opportunity meets preparation. Preparation in leadership for Women of Colour is training and executing your plan with wit and mastery. The secret to high performance individuals is their desire to be curious and test perceived boundaries and assumptions. This is the type of training we need to engage in, the kind that forces us to clear out the cobwebs of false narratives, oppressive political constructs, limiting beliefs, negative mindsets and fears and trauma. You deserve nothing less than the success that is meaningful to you and I know that with the right tools, support, training and strategic plan you can succeed.

Your map to warrior leadership

This is your map to becoming a warrior Woman of Colour leader that transforms the world. My invitation to you is to commit to warrior regardless of where you may think you are on the Women of Colour leadership journey map.

Mindset		Focus
Warrior		Self transcendence
Leader		Leverage
Cadet		Self actualisation
Dreamer		Action
Follower		Decision
Sufferer		Acceptance

Women of Colour leadership journey map

The first column (to the left titled mindset) is where we are currently at, it is the action we are currently taking in life that exemplifies our current mindset. Remember, this is about what our current action tells us about our mindset and does not label our identity. It is our mindset that dictates our actions, daily choices that add up and determine our outcomes, experiences and results in our career and leadership journey. Warriors act and behave as warriors, cadets as cadets, followers as followers and so on. When we choose to think, feel, act and behave at these levels, this in turn is the impact our actions have on our lives, our growth, our families, our communities, in our sisterhood and out in the world. Identifying at which level you are in this column requires rigorous honesty. This is something that only you and you alone can answer. The next column is focus and this is what you need to hone your attention on at each step in the journey. For example, for a follower to step–up to the next level (dreamer) they must focus on decision. If you are currently a cadet then self–actualisation is the focus area that will take you to the next level (leader).

When we map ourselves, we need to be very honest with where we currently are in our leadership journey; the place we are currently leading and living from every day. Where we place ourselves on the map is not about what we have experienced in the past or where we want to be but where we currently are. It has everything to do with how we're choosing to think and to importantly behave at this present moment. Of course, there are situations that we have no control over that traumatise and discriminate against us and against our will that have resulted in us being where we are in life and career. But we all have the choice to heal from it and define what our experience is going to be of our own lives from that point forward and what we do with those situations, how we process and respond to the trauma.

Remember that mindset dictates action and action is not just what we do, but also what we are choosing to think, feel and say consciously unconsciously and subconsciously. Everything is a choice, an action. What do your current actions say about you and where your current mindset and therefore healing is at? Let's unpack the leadership map in a bit more detail.

Sufferer

When I was creating this model based on my years of experience working with Women of Colour, I wanted this word to be strong enough to instigate you to be anything but. Many of us come from cultures that experienced slavery because of colonisation and some of us may still have a strong emotional and physical reaction to words such as 'slave' and 'slavery.' Quite a few of us are now living in western countries where slavery has been (for the most part) condemned and people who look and sound like us are no longer viewed as or forced into slavery by the perceived majority. What we as Women of Colour have become are people who have suffered from systemic discrimination and its effects.

While we may be free from physical slavery, we remain bound by the psychological shackles of a new kind of modern-day slavery.

#ColourFULL

Being victims of the system and experiencing the effects of unhealed discrimination and trauma has us in a mode of perpetual suffering that manifests from the inside out. Many of us are told to do the office housework or expected to, despite holding managerial or senior roles. We experience office politics, suppressors who unfortunately work tirelessly to ensure we are limited to only work at a certain level or area, removed of our decision-making power and responsibilities and opportunities, as well as playing games to get us fired, demoted or performance-managed out of our role. We have also become enslaved to an internalised oppression of daily challenges and interference, aggravated by the effects of ancestral, intergenerational and collective trauma, colonisation, discrimination, racism and our own trauma. Manifesting as limiting beliefs and mindsets, fears, negative emotions, societal and cultural expectations, pressures and beliefs we think feel, behave and act from a place of suffering. As a result, we withhold showing up in the world and our own potential, we judge and negatively treat our sisters who may look slightly different, have a lighter or darker skin tone to us or who have more success and opportunities. Perhaps we may even engage in unintentional or intentional lateral violence of varying degrees not just to our sisters, but to ourselves.

It takes inner fitness to come against systemic discrimination and racism and speak and act out against it, rather than believe what the oppressor says and take it on as our narrative and story. As people say, if you don't write and tell your story, someone else will do it for you. The same is true of your future, particularly for Women of Colour. Nina Simone said, 'You feel the shame, humiliation, and anger at being just another victim of prejudice, and at the same time, there's the nagging worry that maybe...you're just no good.' Heartbreaking isn't it, when you think of yourself as a little girl with all your dreams and goals, believing now that she is 'no good.'

Regardless of what you have endured, you have the power and freedom of choice to go on the path of healing and in the process refuse to take on the narrative that you are a victim, freeing yourself and therefore your potential and ability to attain your leadership goals from the inside out. History is littered with examples of Women of Colour who have overcome extreme circumstances to create freedom and financial prosperity. These are the women we must look up to as role models for a blueprint on how to advance as a Woman of Colour despite the internal and external barriers and challenges. They offer inspiration to keep going and to free ourselves from the grips of systemic discrimination and racism. You must find those stories, treasure them and hold them close to you at all times. Use them as frameworks and a blueprint to free yourself from the suffering of internalised oppression.

When we don't choose to take the time to self–preserve, to heal, to reclaim our power and instead stay a victim and suffer from our internalised oppression day in day out, our internal pain and suffering keeps those with power in power; fuelling them to keep doing what they've always done for all the wrong reasons. It reinforces weak narratives about who Women of Colour are, our future, our potential, the lives we lead, our individual and collective power and the achievements that we have and will accomplish. And so, our pain and suffering affirms, validates and fuels them to continue their barbaric behaviour to our sisters, daughters, aunties, mothers, colleagues, friends and generations to come. Every action we take produces a negative impact, a deficit. We take one step forward resulting in us ending up 10 steps back. This is because our action stems from a mindset of suffering; internalised suppression. You may find yourself saying there are certain things that we cannot change and this is true, there are things outside our control that we cannot change, but through strategy and masterful execution of the things that are within our control we can overcome some of these perceived barriers, freeing ourselves in the process from internalised oppression and pushing back on systemic discrimination and racism to become powerful leaders that transform the world.

Be the generation that says 'no more.' Nothing creates change and freedom quite like a revolution. A bold courageous decision and a commitment to no longer be a victim of your suffering and internalised oppression. The deep intensive and consistent work to self–preserve, heal and develop anti–fragility and resilience. In their revolution and through their rigorous commitment to action and their future, the people not only set themselves and others free in the process but they also reclaim their power, empower themselves and possibly those generations to come. Give yourself permission to create freedom by being who you have always been called to be, by being who you always knew you were deep down regardless of the false narratives that swirl inside your mind (side note: being your fullest and most authentic version of yourself does not excuse unethical, unlawful or bad behaviour!) This to me is true freedom from systemic discrimination: when we are no longer choosing to live from a place of suffering and victim mentality; when we have healed from our resentments, fears, anger and trauma we are no longer dictated, bound, oppressed or imprisoned by them and this frees our potential, unlocking our talents and gifts as well as our ability to show up as the fullest versions of ourselves and unleash our inner warrior leader. Choose to live and lead unapologetically and unashamedly as you are. This is in itself revolutionary. Life is short. Make the one you have count.

So how do we do this? The action you need to take to go to the next level in the Women of Colour leadership journey map is acceptance. Accept that suffering is no longer working for you. Accept that you have no control over the things you cannot control or change, accept that you have the ability to change the things of which you have power to change (those that are in your control) and work to develop the wisdom to see the difference between the two. Accept that this is a journey that requires you to do the unsexy, deeply uncomfortable and often hard and challenging work to self–preserve, heal, free yourself from internalised oppression and step into your potential, who you always knew you were deep down, unapologetically and unashamedly. Accept that this journey was never promised to be easy but it is promised to be worth it. Accept that you have the power to live life and lead as a warrior Woman of Colour and accept that you deserve to attain what your heart and soul most desires. You deserve to be a powerful leader that transforms the world. Accept that the way you have been living and approaching your career, business and or leadership journey just isn't working for you anymore and that you need a fresh start which may be uncomfortable for a little while.

Accept that your negative thoughts, emotions, false narratives, fears, limiting beliefs and behaviours are no longer serving you and need to be let go of with love, tenderness, pure surrender and grace.

#ColourFULL

Accept that you have drifted away from who you truly are and your purpose. Accept that you need to show up in a greater capacity, more fully and or in a different way and give yourself permission to put yourself first and pursue what you want to pursue in your life, career and or business unapologetically and unashamedly. Acceptance is the first action we need to take in our leadership journey. Accept the inner warrior that is sitting inside you, waiting for you, dear sister, to set them free so that they can free and heal you and others while transforming the world.

Follower

My dog Bubbles follows me everywhere. I have a small house that is open plan and simple in layout but no matter where I go, even to the toilet, Bubbles follow me. As I type this sentence, he is in my home office with me, sleeping on my lap. Followers are great at taking massive action and working extremely hard but are often not applying themself to what they truly want to do or engaging in meaningful work and tasks that provide them with freedom through self-expression. Essentially, they're not doing what they want to do with their life and may not even know what they truly want to do. Followers waste their talent and potential in the pursuit of other people's dreams and expectations because it's easier. They may work for the oppressor, fuelling, affirming and validating their efforts, or they may be working for someone and doing a job that leaves them feeling unfulfilled and disgruntled at the end of the day. Followers create and experience negative and deficit impact for themselves. Every step they take is essentially going backwards because the steps are not their own. They are simply following others because of the denial of self.

The key word here is decision. At this level, we make a non-negotiable decision to not be a follower and instead to do the hard, uncomfortable and often ugly work of stripping away false narratives and limiting beliefs to get to the essence of who we are and therefore our path. We make a decision to not be a follower who fulfils other people's dreams and expectations of us; we make a decision to create our own path to unlock and unleash our inner warrior who has decided to push the perceived boundaries of our human potential unapologetically and unashamedly.

Dreamer

Dreams do not come true, people do. A dreamer is someone who has evolved their thinking but chooses to stay in the familiarity and comfort of victim mode. Dreamers are people with secret dreams and desires. I call dreamers the Oprah fans; they will devour every piece of content there is, do every free course and webinar, collect and like all the #inspo posts, read all the right books and talk the talk but ultimately lack the action of walking the walk. When you ask them why they're not pursuing their dreams or living up to their potential, they have a million rational excuses and logical justifications. One of the most common excuses I hear when providing leadership support to Women of Colour is, 'I need to get clear and think it through myself first.' Or, 'I don't have enough time,' 'I'm not ready yet,' 'I have carer responsibilities,' 'I'm not sure, I'll have to think about it,' 'It's too much money,' the list goes on and on. These are all plausible and rational reasons. Sometimes this hesitation comes from not wanting to waste my time as a professional but let me make something very clear: this is the exact purpose of an expert, coach and mentor, to help you get unstuck and to hold you accountable to the decisions and actions that you need to be taking. Life wasn't meant to be forged alone and working with a skilled coach can get you further so much faster while ensuring you feel supported in the process.

At this level you will experience zero impact: for every step you take, you will remain exactly at that step. For dreamers, this is not new news. To move forward and create traction towards leadership goals and success, dreamers must shift their mindset from consumption to action. Sister, we need loads of action. For dreamers to move into a cadet mindset and to go to the next level in the Women of Colour leadership journey map, the focus is action, and the first action they must take is to remove themselves from playing the excuse and justification card, the narrative they keep repeating to themselves, and step into a new story; the story they always knew they wanted deep down but were fearful to admit, invite in and accept. Basically, the complete opposite story of any excuse or justification they were playing on repeat before. The commitment here is to take action before you're ready, before you feel motivated and to be ok without seeing immediate returns, outcomes and results. It's the hard and uncomfortable work of getting you unstuck from the excuses and justifications of victim mentality to heal your wounds, glean wisdom from them and take a purposeful step into your personal power. When we take consistent, massive action we can prove to ourselves and our communities with evidence that those oppressive narratives are false. We disempower the oppressor and give permission to our sisters to do the same. We weren't meant to be dreamers; we were born to be leaders and warriors.

We were born to be people who stand up to the system and say, 'no more.'

#ColourFULL

People who take the massive action needed to turn dreams into realities. When we do, we start to weaken the very system that holds us and our sisters back. We refuse to stay stuck and suppressed and we remove our psychological shackles, taking charge of our futures and refusing to succumb to others' lesser expectations.

Dreamers know what to do, how to do it and why. They just need to get on with doing it. Confidence and motivation come through action, not the other way around. So, don't wait to feel ready, confident or motivated. Start now, start today.

Cadet

A cadet is someone who is in a season of preparation and training for the position or responsibility they are about to take on. Their sole job at this level is simply to train, train again and then train some more usually under the guidance of a leader, teacher mentor or coach. They position themselves as a student eager to learn, surrendering to the process and working the training program. They eat, breathe and sleep their training. Training can be so rigorous and challenging that at times they may feel like giving up but if they maintain their intensity, they get to see what is possible and to go beyond the perceived limits of their potential. Training is also a full–time job. During this intense period of learning, what cadets speak, feel and think consistently on a daily basis is the future that awaits them. Every action they choose is an act of integrity to themselves. Every action demonstrates and confirms to their subconscious, unconscious and conscious mind that they have and are keeping up the commitment to reach for that goal of warrior leadership, to become that leader and fulfil their potential, because they deserve it. Where your focus goes, your energy goes and energy plus actions produces results.

This to me is what self–belief is: self–trust. Trust yourself to make the commitment to fulfilling your wildest dreams and greatest potential. Keep the commitments you make to yourself regardless of whether you feel like it or not so that you build a deep internal knowing that you will show up for yourself no matter what. Cadets must learn build their personal integrity: the ability and mindset to honour oneself with love, integrity and respect. Self–belief and self–trust are only achieved through rigorous, continuous and consistent action. Let's rephrase this quote from James Clear, 'Every action you take is a vote for the type of person you wish to become. No single instance will transform your beliefs, but as the votes build up, so does the evidence of your new identity.' (James Clear, *Atomic Habits*, 2018). Instead, we can say, 'For Women of Colour, every action we take today is a vote for the future we want to create for ourselves; a vote towards our commitment to do what it takes to achieve our goals and be the leader that we always knew we were deep down. Every action we take is a gift we know we deserve to give to ourselves. The gift of living unapologetically and unashamedly as who we truly are, fulfilling our greatest potential and becoming a powerful leader that transforms the world.' At the cadet level, it is common for all the fears and self–limiting beliefs that you have to surface to the top – an unravelling and unveiling of the true you that had been stripped down and eaten away by life. This is unsettling, unfamiliar. It's almost as if we don't know this person, the real us and this makes us feel uncertain. It's this uncertainty that fuels and gives rise to fear and it is fear that creates limiting beliefs. This is the tipping point and the deciding moment of whether you slip back down through the levels of the warrior leadership journey map or decide to persist daily with your efforts to challenge all of your fears and self–limiting beliefs to breakthrough and rebirth the leader you always knew you were deep down inside.

To pass through this level, what you need is declaration. Declare the leader that you are, demand its calling into fruition and into life like Jesus raising Lazarus up from the dead. Call and command the person you were created to be back to life. You don't need a miracle; you are your own miracle. Daily declarations realign our emotions and thinking to our vision and create personal power. No longer allow yourself permission to submit to negative thoughts, feelings, limiting beliefs, fears and trauma. These are like weeds. When you think you have gotten rid of them all, another one pops up and their roots are long, running deep and tough to pull out if you let them grow too big. Prevention is better than cure so stay inner fit and build that self–trust and self–belief to stay on the path to warrior leadership.

The key word here to move you to the next level of the Women of Colour leadership journey map is self–actualisation. When you reach the tipping point it's like a pressure cooker about to go off and that's when we know we are so close to self–actualisation, to rebirth, if only we would breathe and keep going. Remember your perceived set back is in fact setting you up for your breakthrough. Self–actualisation gives you a different level of maturity, a deep awareness and understanding of who you are, your purpose, limits and potential. You understand you can achieve anything with intense self–belief and consistent, unwavering confidence in yourself regardless of any chitter–chatter that may surface in your mind. If it does, you have the psychological fitness to observe it and gently ask it to leave acknowledging that this stinking thought or feeling no longer serves your highest self. Self–actualisation comes through hardship, sweat, extreme discomfort and sometimes tears. It is the result of endurance, stamina, anti–fragility and resilience built over time in one's long, intense and challenging training journey. If you can safely think back to your most traumatic and painful past life experiences, you will notice that these are the times you usually have truly gotten to know and understand yourself and your capabilities on a richer and deeper level. Defining moments when you experienced fear but doggedly pushed through and proved to yourself that those fears were false; stepping forward, building self–belief and self–trust. You can do this again; you have already proven to yourself that you have what it takes, it was always there. Commit, believe, trust, declare and action.

Leader

Leaders can be anyone. You can be an exceptional leader as a mother and auntie, a sister or friend; you can lead an organisation, a community or a group; you can be an activist or simply someone who wants to be a good person. A leader is someone that leverages their influence, and that is the focus at this level. I was once asked by a young Woman of Colour what it felt like to be a leader and if you are able to relax when you are at the 'top.' I told her that it was the complete opposite, that what I found I was doing day in day out was giving of myself to others. As executives in a traditional organisation structure, we are constantly putting out fires and solving problems for the organisation, our people and for ourselves. We support and care for the people around us. At this level we need to be very strategic about who we form relationships with and why.

Leadership starts with self. How can you lead others if you cannot lead yourself through your darkest life experiences? Healing is integral to leadership and is the first step in being a leader as a Woman of Colour. To graduate to a leader you must have mastered self–leadership and done the deep work to heal past wounds. If we do not have the proper training to heal from our wounds, we are not able to leverage our influence effectively or in a safe way to the people we serve. We could jeopardise their physical, psychological and cultural safety. As a Thought Leader in the advancement of Women of Colour, I realised very early on that I needed to be very careful about whom I shared my stage with. After a few experiences with Women of Colour who seemed to have kind, generous and honest intentions turned unpleasant, I realised that their energy could either nurture or pollute my community and that I was ultimately responsible for that by way of choosing to put them on 'stage.' Quality of leadership energy results from the degree of healing that has occurred in our wounds and determines whether we are leaders who influence to nurture or to pollute (whether intentionally or unintentionally). I now pay less attention to people's achievements and am more attuned to their energy to intuitively seek out healed individuals.

\#

We must lead 'From our scars and not from our wounds' for the safety of those we influence.

#ColourFULL

Inner fitness training enables us to manage the energy we carry, the emotions and wounds we hold and heal to take 100% responsibility for ourselves and others.

The key word here to move us to the next level on the Women of Colour leadership journey map is leverage. Our biggest asset is ourselves. A real leader knows this and does not rely solely on their board, boss, manager or people to provide them with opportunities to develop, lead and to grow as a warrior leader. They proactively seek them out. As a leader we are evolving and growing and learning, unlearning and relearning by putting our continuous training to use. At this level, leadership training must not stop. Seek out and engage mentors and executives or business coaches to provide you with expertise and feedback, advise you on the areas that you need to develop, be your sounding board and keep you in check. Leadership can oftentimes feel lonely and when things don't work out the finger is usually pointed at you first, so anti–fragility and resilience through inner fitness (emotional, intellectual, psychological and spiritual strength) is vital at this level. A mentor and or coach will help you train and build your anti–fragility and resilience, like a muscle that continues to flex and break down on a daily basis to become stronger and stronger over time. Leadership is not just about the power to influence but the honour and blessing to leverage our influence and serve others for the betterment of our people, cultures and our communities. The title of a leader is one that is earned and given to you by the people you serve. It is one that you seek to earn every single day by the thoughts that you think, the feelings you feel, the words that you say and the actions that you take. Leadership is not a title or throne. Leadership is hard work and responsibility. We are all created to be leaders but it requires consistent, rigorous daily training and laser–like focus. Be a leader that people want to follow by being a leader that you would want to follow first. Leverage your influence.

Warrior

A warrior is someone who takes 100% responsibility for their life and does not engage in excuses, justifications, the blame game or sit in anger, negative emotions or thoughts, fear, limiting beliefs, resentment or anger (or at least not for very long). They strategise, plan and train to execute their strategy masterfully to the best of their ability. When they fail, they persist. They create a new plan, tweak their training and go again with a harder, faster and deeper intensity and focus. Being a warrior is not about whether you have hustle or not; it's about how you hustle. I've met plenty of women who have fancy LinkedIn profiles and three businesses plus a full–time job. From this, it's easy to assume that they are hustling and are warriors but what's really going on is a survival mindset. With enough poking and provoking, I can crack the glass case and see that underneath is a very broken, confused person who is doing 101 things because they are in survival mode, a desperate search to find something that will 'work' and propel them into leadership success.

Warriors have incredible focus; they have a strategy and a plan but will only flex and pivot if evidence shows that they need to. They are 100% focused on the process and loosely hold onto the outcome being agile and adaptable to opportunities along the way. Their focus is not the ego or glory of warrior leadership but the consuming process of serving, improving and optimising: self–transcendence. They are on a journey to get better and better; to conquer again and again, push the boundaries and stretch possibilities and transform the world through a spiritual connection. Glory is not the driver. The pursuit of freedom for their people and themselves is, and they stay unwaveringly committed to the process. More on this soon...

*Share the quotes in this chapter with others
so that they too can be elevated, empowered and inspired.*

*Remember to tag Winitha so that we can reshare
your post with our global community.*
Turn to p274 for Winitha's social media handles.

2

Choice:
the power is ours

"If you look at what you have in life, you'll always have more. If you look at what you don't have in life, you'll never have enough."

~ Oprah Winfrey

As a Thought Leader and entrepreneur, my work is founded in facts, research, science and numbers. However, like many Women of Colour, I also have a very strong spiritual side to me. So please, bear with me and know that I am not trying to 'love and light' anything away. Your experiences, emotions and current reality are true and real. You are true and real. In this chapter, all I'm offering is an alternative way of interacting with the world around you because in business, career and my personal life I've had way too many experiences where approaching people, places and situations with a spiritual lens has transformed my life in a way that theory, science and facts could not. I know this to also be true for the many smart and clever Women of Colour leaders I've coached, mentored, interviewed and researched around the world.

Those of you who are professional dancers will know that a key challenge in dance is remembering the choreography. Memorising lines is one thing but getting your body to remember movement is another. I started dancing at around 20 years old and in the early days my greatest struggle was in remembering the choreography. Finally, I considered that maybe the reason why I couldn't remember was because I kept telling myself that I couldn't. I thought...what if I told myself, every day, that I had a freaking awesome memory and that I always remember the choreography; every class, every time – even when in reality I did actually forget? So, I did. I stood at the centre front (a vulnerable place to position yourself in a dance class!) and eyeballed myself in the mirror and told myself, every dance class, that I had an excellent memory. I believed it and acted as if it were reality. Of course, it was no magic instant pill. At the beginning, I was challenged to keep acting as if: visualising, saying and feeling the emotion of having achieved it even when I did actually stuff up and forget. I had to pick myself up off the floor – literally sometimes! – dust myself off, hit reset and try again. And over time, things started to change. Since then, I have never found remembering choreography a challenge. Even now. A few weeks ago, I did an online dance class and I was nervous about picking up the choreography as it had been two or three years since I last danced. I set my intention, acted as if and...I picked it up. This kind of positive outcome is thanks to the hours of psychological (inner) fitness training I have done over the years to create a new neural pathway in my brain. Basically, I had replaced a false belief that harmed me (that I had a bad memory) with a new one that helped me (that I had a great memory). I did this by focusing intensely and consistently on the experience I wanted to create as opposed to the one I was experiencing: a false narrative that was holding me back from realising and fulfilling my potential.

There are so many stories around the world of People of Colour from when time began to this day, who have overcome extreme circumstances, discrimination and trauma because they decided – chosen – to shift their thoughts and emotions and refuse to accept their current reality as their future. These examples show us again and again that the impossible is possible. Things (that are in our sphere of control) are only impossible if we choose to perceive them that way. This may annoy some but I do believe that where there is a will there's a way and that my life and those of other successful Women of Colour leaders past to present are a continuous testimony to this. As Women of Colour, we just need to find a way through and that, in my experience, can be done by tapping into your personal power; shifting your thoughts and feelings, healing, self–preservation, taking massive action that aligns to what you do want and having the tools and strategies to navigate and manage White systems.

The Law of Attraction states that what we think and feel is what we draw into our life. Obviously, this applies to everything outside of systemic discrimination, oppression and racism, trauma of all degrees and things that are outside of our control. There is a strange energy about this world; you know when you have déjà vu? When you drive around expecting a car park and you get one? When you think about someone and then they call you? To some extent I believe in the Law of Attraction and see elements of its existence in most of our cultural and ancestral spiritual beliefs and practices, which speak to the connection between thoughts, emotions, action, results and possibility. The Law of Attraction is a simple tool that we Women of Colour can use to create opportunities for us to advance. I firmly believe that if we start collectively declaring our brilliance, greatness and potential; start declaring a new reality for ourself and our sisters, that things will shift and collectively we will become powerful leaders that transform the world. Now, this is no bullshit. It is the natural law of life that governs this world. What we think, say and feel, we call into being. So, use your words, thoughts and feelings to create the life that you want – the key is taking aligned action. Negative stuff happens – that's life – but name it, feel it, explore it and talk it through with a mentor, coach or psychologist for guidance and support as you walk through it. Then, when you're ready, get to the work of declaring that you are healed, prosperous and brilliant; that you are receiving that job, that business growth, that love into your life and get to work in taking action that aligns to your declaration. Don't give into negative feelings and emotions. Don't feed the energy that keeps systemic discrimination and racism alive.

Freedom won't come to you from anyone else but yourself. It comes from actively creating your own reality and going for what you want. Unfortunately, this is the world we live in. If we wait for equity and equality, we will be waiting our whole lives and to do so acknowledges, verifies and affirms that we are indeed powerless and that White folk and men have all the power and that, in essence, we are at the mercy of non–Women of Colour. Michelle Obama said that she doesn't wait for equality and I agree, so too do the Women of Colour leaders I have interviewed, researched and talked to who have been able to advance and achieve success. They refuse to accept the reality that others create or try and force us to accept and instead create their own.

At a simple psychological level, we know the power our thoughts, feelings and emotions have and the impact they make on the actions we take: the way that we respond to situations and people and the outcomes resulting from those interactions. I think a simple example of what the Law of Attraction is, is...energy. I'm no expert, like everyone I'm just curious about how this world works and the connection between energy, spirituality, reality and possibility. All I know from repeated personal experience is that there is a certain energy force that governs us and this world. We can use it for good or we can use it for bad but it is there ready for us to tap into. Richard Bach said, 'Argue for your limitations and, sure enough, they're yours.' In other words, we get what we fight for, that which we invest our actions, thoughts and feelings into. To win the outcome you do want, choose actions and thoughts that rally against your negative emotions and all those nasty thoughts that hold you back. Every action thought and emotion you invite in is creating your reality, so choose the ones that create the reality you actually want. Give up fighting for mediocrity and instead choose to fight for your success. The choice is entirely yours.

Science is only at the brink of understanding the connection between mind and body. I read about a study that was conducted on athletes that discovered that the athletes' muscles would react when they visualised themselves performing. Like many of us, I was made to learn classical piano as a child. Before going to sleep in the nights leading up to exams, I would listen to cassette tapes of professionals playing my music exam pieces and visualise myself playing it as perfectly as they did. I saw through my own eyes, me in my body looking at my hands and the keyboard and with every note I played perfectly I felt all the emotions of joy, success and happiness that came with my achievement. Visualising just before you go to sleep is one of the most powerful things you can do to attract and bring your dreams and goals to fruition because of the state your mind is in as you sleep. The mind controls the body, not the other way around. Tell the body what you want it to do repeatedly and it'll eventually get the point and follow your command.

The heart's magnetic field is 60 times stronger than the brain and can be measured up to several feet away from the body. Thinking alone is not sufficient.

#ColourFULL

Your feelings are stronger than thoughts in creating your reality and what you want in life. There is no point saying affirmations repeatedly or thinking new thoughts if your feelings are not aligned. Work equally hard, if not 60 times more to ensure your feelings are vibrating loud and clearly and aligned to what you think and say (inside and out loud).

Now, let's flip this a little. Shifting our thoughts or feelings alone without action will be fruitless. Neuroscience tells us that to shift our mind, habits, emotions and behaviours in a powerful way, for example by building new ones, we need to start first with behaviours and actions. Thoughts and feelings alone will not do it. For example, just thinking you are healthy and fit is not going to magically make you healthy and fit. It takes the actions of eating properly and working out to make that a reality. Action is the secret sauce to actualising the Law of Attraction: actions that align to our intentions in order to call our desired goal or dream into fruition and be attracted into our careers and lives. If you want to take it up a notch, then feel the emotions with the actions (such as I did when I was listening to my piano exam pieces). Thoughts and visualisation are the beginning step to get you started and ignited on your path to shift your inner world so you can make change in your outer world – an integral part of the journey to warrior leadership. When you take action, generate the positive emotions that come with achieving your goal while staying present and wholly focused on the process. Be agile, holding the outcome loosely but with intention, as you take action and work through the process. Choose thoughts and emotions that align to the outcome you want. The choice is entirely ours and this is what it means to have personal power: the freedom and power of choice.

The choice is yours, today. The choice to succeed and not fall into the big hole of oppression, discrimination and suppression. It's a choice no one talks about because they (the oppressor) don't want you to know. Because for you to know that you actually have the power means that you just might succeed in life and become a leader, that you might depower them and tip them off their perch. They want you and your sisters and the next generation and the generation after that to lose all of their power, to be powerless and the easiest way to do this is to make you believe that you are. This is why we are constantly attacked – it's a tactic that's used to wear you down to render you powerless. I also often wonder about the language that is used around concepts like White supremacy and White power and privilege, which can at times negatively impact us on the receiving end internally and externally. Talking to a highly successful First Nations academic, she commented on how having constant conversations and focus on White people and how they are more supreme and have more power and privilege immediately disempowers us by perpetuating and amplifying the energy and focus around it, and therefore how this language must be used sparsely by us as Black, Brown, First Nations and Women of Colour. She also commented on how she believed that the terminology was misleading and problematic for us. It's the reinforcement of a political and social construct that does not serve us even though it's an important and very much needed conversation to have, bringing with it a need to put terminology around it. Lastly, she also commented on how constantly thinking, feeling and having conversations, let alone doing work solely in that area is in itself inequity. The focus, time, energy and resources are entirely or majority on them, and not on us. It made me wonder what would happen if we instead had a conversation about what we as Women of Colour needed, how powerful we are, our potential, possibilities, our future and excellence.

> *Sister, you stand on the shoulders of your ancestors – you are the product of everything they fought for, worked for, believed in, dreamed and hoped. You have their revolutionary blood running through your veins.*
>
> **#ColourFULL**

So choose today to start pushing back, choose to ask for what you deserve and need, choose to not let their words infiltrate your mind body and soul, choose to stand back up again, choose to speak up, choose to stand out, choose self–acceptance, self–preservation, self–belief, choose to lean into challenges and discomfort, choose to turn hardship into opportunity, choose to be psychologically, emotionally, intellectually and spiritually fit, choose to heal, choose to stand in solidarity with your sisters and back them up. Choose to not let the oppressors' false narratives and idiotic behaviour get anywhere close to you, and flush that shit down the toilet.

You are the potential of what is yet to come, the leader we've been waiting for, the leader the world needs. You, dear sister, are the one with the power. Be the creator and master of your world. You freaking deserve it.

*Share the quotes in this chapter with others
so that they too can be elevated, empowered and inspired.*

*Remember to tag Winitha so that we can reshare
your post with our global community.*
Turn to p274 for Winitha's social media handles.

3

Potential: our revolt and revolution

"You can be a thousand different women. It's your choice which one you want to be. It's about freedom and sovereignty. You celebrate who you are. You say, 'This is my kingdom."

~ Salma Hayek

In my years of research into the advancement of Women of Colour, the one thing that keeps coming up over and over again is our relationship with the system that holds us back and what actually holds us back. Stereotyping of Women of Colour can happen before we open our mouths. All sorts of ugly attacks get thrown our way. For example, Women of Colour get labelled passive–aggressive because they have chosen to speak out in a meeting, to their manager, to an idiot or labelled as dramatic because they have complained about racism. This is the collision of gender and cultural discrimination at its best work. Sometimes, even when we are super prepared and skilled in our communication or behave totally masculine or White, we still face judgement and labelling. These attacks have worn us down. Tired and exhausted we give in, we stop speaking out for years, sometimes a lifetime. We get silenced and stay stagnant in our career.

I would say that I am a calm, patient, tolerant and grounded individual but when something aggravates or triggers me, I can be like a ticking timebomb and in that moment, I am graceless, a blubbering hot mess. For me, speaking up has been challenging and very difficult after repeated trauma from truckloads of gaslighting throughout my personal and professional life, trauma in my personal life, being tone–policed and silenced in the boardroom and labelled passive–aggressive more times than you've gone to the toilet this year. I've been gaslighted repeatedly by Women of Colour too but if I can speak up, fall down and get up to speak up again, I know you can too.

It is only by speaking our truth that we can give ourselves the opportunity to see and fully realise our potential and importantly, to heal and reclaim back our power.

#ColourFULL

We may think that pursuing our goals, applying for that job or finally starting that business is pursuing potential but really, our potential is most expanded and achieved when we are at a crossroads; when we are at our most fearful, pressured, challenged and experiencing the most difficulty, stress, exhaustion and wounds. The moments when we feel like giving up and giving in. It is in that crucial moment, where we can so easily give in and accept defeat, that we can instead heal, keep going, increase and leverage our momentum and achieve and realise our fullest potential. Pushing beyond your perceived limitations allows you to witness the miracle of knowing what you are truly made of, your potential and who you truly are. There's no awards, applause, cheers and congratulations, but there is opportunity to grow, transform, heal and see the evidence of your potential.

A few years ago, I left a role in an organisation that was diseased with discrimination, bullying and sexual harassment. I had just endured a gruelling six months of working my arse off on top of performance managing the CEO myself to get him fired for the trauma he caused others and myself when I realised the board did nothing after I formally complained three months prior. What I learned during those six months was the importance of speaking up and the power and freedom of protection it gave to all the others who had gone before me who didn't have a voice, and those coming after who haven't found theirs yet. In my next position, I found myself working as a consultant for a business that had a team of people who had formed a boys' club. I was patient, tolerant and calm while I quietly observed how they continuously left me out of key conversations with clients, meetings, emails and high–level projects. What I really wanted to do in that moment was to call the CEO and give him a piece of my mind but if I had learned anything from the previous organisation, it was that I needed to strategise and craft a plan, keep it close to me and always to be two steps ahead. These situations are, to me, like playing a game of chess. I had been keeping written notes and documenting issues and incidents since the boys' club behaviour started. I dedicated a couple of days to healing, thinking, strategising and planning before reaching out to my executive coach to book in an urgent session. She had been kept up to date on the situation and was someone external who could be rational and pragmatic when exploring the issues with me. In our meeting, we went over my notes and the situation and discussed my plan – what was in my best interest, not theirs. For good record keeping and to maintain some distance from the confrontation (considering I was quite triggered emotionally) we agreed the best approach was to send the CEO a clear and concise, factual email detailing my grievances and a proposed solution. I drafted the email, sent it to my executive coach for feedback and then emailed it to him. We both knew he wouldn't meet the proposed solution let alone agree that there was a problem and so I decided in advance that I would leave the position before he made a passive–aggressive move. We decided that the most important thing for me in that moment was to stand up, speak out and self–preserve but to not engage in the drama. This wasn't about him or the other idiots, it was about me. I chose to view the situation as an opportunity for me to flex my speaking–up muscles and I did in a way that was empowering to me; all about me, not about him.

That situation and how I dealt with it was very different to how I would have dealt with it in the past. In the past, I would have kept silent and cried secret tears; feeling sorry for myself and putting up with it until I had a mental breakdown and then left the role. The truth is, even though it was hard and I was already exhausted and wounded from the previous job, I used my voice to speak out because I knew that, in that moment, I wasn't alone. I had all my sisters and ancestors there with me in the room, supporting and holding space for me. I knew that I was stronger than what I felt at the time. My past experiences informed my inner being that I could do it, I was stronger than my emotions and that my voice was valid and had power. I was powerful beyond what I felt in that moment. I also knew that it was important for me to reclaim my power in that situation and all those that had preceded it when I hadn't spoken out – in that moment I reclaimed my power from the actions of that idiot and others in the workplace and also from all the times in my career, business and life where I didn't speak out due to the trauma and pain. Reclaiming my power in that moment was an important part of my healing from those past experiences.

It is in the grimy, messy, often chaotic and gruelling times of hardship that we have the opportunity to realise what we are truly made of. It's how diamonds are made and how leaders that change the world are born. These situations are a training ground for your greatness and your future leadership; the success you are about to achieve. They are a training ground for what God or the universe has called you to do – the work that is required of you to impact, influence and truly change the world for yourself, your community, the sisterhood and the next generation. So, lean into these challenging times, dear sister, because the greatest gift we receive from them is anti–fragility: we become stronger because of it (Nassim Nicholas Taleb, *Anti-fragile: Things that Gain from Disorder,* 2012). Resilience is pushing against trials and tribulations to make it through, but anti–fragility is about stepping into those situations to regain control and power. We get stronger, flourish and thrive as a result of moving through the tension and in fact, we need it to gain a competitive edge.

Do it for your ancestors whose voices were silenced by colonisation. Do it for all our future generations so organisations and their leaders know that it isn't ok to treat Woman of Colour as irrelevant and disposable, that we will no longer stand for it; that they can expect a revolt from Women of Colour, a reclaiming of our power through substantial action against them and their diseased organisations and to know that collectively we are creating a revolution in our careers, life and businesses and for ourselves, our cultures and community. It is only by speaking our truth that we can give ourselves the opportunity to see and fully realise our potential and give permission for others to also do the same. This is how warrior leaders are birthed and how revolutions are started. Start yours today and ensure you have support around you as you enact and activate your revolt. Change your mindset, view these challenging times as gifts to strengthen your anti–fragility muscle. Seize the opportunity for hardship to become your greatest achievement and source of strength. The achievement of your potential to become a truly powerful leader that transforms the world.

Share the quotes in this chapter with others
so that they too can be elevated, empowered and inspired.

Remember to tag Winitha so that we can reshare
your post with our global community.
Turn to p274 for Winitha's social media handles.

4

Imposter syndrome: the truth behind it

"Finally I was able to see that if I had a contribution I wanted to make, I must do it, despite what others said. That I was OK the way I was. That it was all right to be strong."

~ Wangari Maathai, 1991 interview with Priscilla Sears

I want to talk to you about an epidemic that is holding Women of Colour like you back from their potential. As a leadership trainer, coach, mentor and expert in this space, I've had so many conversations with Women of Colour around the world. We talk about their dreams, what's in their heart and how they can strategise to overcome their internal barriers and external challenges to advance in their career and business. The one phrase that comes up repeatedly in our conversations is imposter syndrome: 'I think I have imposter syndrome,' 'Maybe I'm thinking like that because of imposter syndrome,' 'I feel anxious because of imposter syndrome...'

Seriously Sis, stop. Enough with the self–diagnosis. Hit pause and let's dive into this a little.

Imposter Syndrome can look differently to different people. For some it's subtle and arises as a feeling of self–doubt, 'Can I do this? I'm not sure I can, that's not really me,' 'I'm not someone who leads others. I am the worker bee,' and my favourite, 'I don't want to be front of stage, that's for other people, I do the work in the background because it's about serving and not being in the limelight.' For many, it's the feeling of being a fraud. That you are just winging it – that you lack the abilities, skills and inner essence to be at your level or work in your role. Feeling that you are simply pretending and that someone will eventually find out that you've been faking it the entire time and you'll be made an absolute fool out of in public! At the heart of it, imposter syndrome is caused by a lack of confidence and serious self–doubt that sabotages your ability to stretch, grow and reach for what you really want. So instead, you stay in your comfort zone, let fear run riot on your life, in your body and drown your soul in excuses and justifications. I know what it feels like, let me share with you my own experience.

When I got my first General Manager (GM) role, I was super excited until two days before my first day when I started feeling sick to my stomach. My body was pulsating in panic. I thought, 'What if I sink the entire ship! What if the company crashes and it's all my fault and everyone knows? What if they find out how stupid I really am?' The mere thought of being a GM made me want to faint let alone the thought of doing something like the CEO role. I wanted to pull out but I'm also a bit of a risk taker so I dove head first into the deep–end, screaming all the way down... Turns out I could do a GM role standing on my head and after a few months into the role, I got bumped into the top job, the CEO position. Funnily enough I made an even incredible CEO too. I achieved more in 12 months than the previous three CEOs had in the last five years. It was all in my damn head. What had I been so scared about? All I needed was an opportunity and action to discover that the fear was all in my head, that it wasn't real at all, and that the truth of who I was and what I was really made of was on the other side of that fear. I simply needed to step to the other side of the road to find out that I made a damn good GM and an even better CEO.

#

We Women of Colour are so far removed from who we really are it's no wonder we feel like imposters.

#ColourFULL

Colonisation, systemic discrimination and racism has affected us in many ways and many of us continue to be bound by its effects – the psychological shackles of White masculine systems and structures. Living in western countries according to the White masculine way or living in a country that has far drifted from our Indigenous roots; we talk, write, dress, work, think, feel, communicate, live, do our hair and make–up, decide, believe and behave in White western masculine ways. On top of this, every day we are bombarded by who we 'should be' by social media and the general media, telling us that we are only beautiful if our skin and hair look a certain way, we are only valid, valued, seen and heard if we talk and behave in a certain way. We are bombarded by content that tells us repeatedly that we are not 'enough' and so we try to be 'enough' in the White western masculine context according to everyone else's definitions and expectations, and end up being someone that may not really be us at all. In the workplace and in business, we are constantly circled by other people's expectations of our work: our ways of doing, how long and at what intensity, what we need to be working on and the results we need to produce. We experience systemic discrimination, suppression, oppression and racism on a daily basis in and outside of work. The glass–ceiling for Women of Colour is double if not triple that of White women. We are being suffocated out of being our true selves. We face the pressure and expectation of cultural and societal beliefs dictated and directed by colonisation. On top of that we experience our own cultural expectations, pressures and dictations of how we should think, feel and behave, we may even inherit ancestral or intergenerational trauma as well as experience patriarchal and matriarchal systems that don't serve our highest good. Tiring just thinking about it all, huh?

My encouragement to you is that when you do feel like an imposter, take a step back and ask yourself, 'Am I being ME right now?' and get back to how you are feeling in your body as opposed to your head. To me, feeling like an imposter isn't about a lack of ability, skills or qualifications but my soul, my inner self waving a red flag saying, 'Winitha...who are you? You've drifted away from who you are. Come back!'

Being called a Woman of Colour is powerful to me. It is about taking back power of the term 'colour' and redefining the narrative around it for yourself and your sisters.

#ColourFULL

Get back to doing you and promise yourself to do only you. Imposter syndrome is a term, it doesn't have to be a diagnosis for life, a label you stick on your forehead everywhere you go or a story you tell when you meet someone new. You get to decide who you are. That feeling inside is simply a little flag waving at you, inviting you to get back to who you are as a Woman of Colour. So Sister, get back to YOU. When you do, you honour yourself with integrity, grace and love and that is something no one can take away from you.

*Share the quotes in this chapter with others
so that they too can be elevated, empowered and inspired.*

*Remember to tag Winitha so that we can reshare
your post with our global community.*
Turn to p274 for Winitha's social media handles.

5

Fear:
when to trust it and when not to

"Never trust your fears...they don't know your strength."

~ Athena Singh

I've been watching my little nephew grow from the day I found out my sister was six weeks pregnant to now as a three–year old. It's profound to see how the body and mind are programmed from conception. He's at the age where he's pretty clear on what he wants and has no buts, ifs or hesitation about it. There is little he is scared of. As a toddler, he has no qualms about speaking in front of others, meeting new kids he doesn't know or reaching for something in a store – regardless of its price tag. It's interesting to compare our adult selves to this past stage of our life and examine the things we are fearful of now that did not paralyse us as kids. A lot of the time, we find the fear has been borne from our past trauma, pain, discrimination, social and cultural conditioning and information consumption.

We all know the psychology behind fear. Our brains are programmed to keep us safe from potential dangers, be it bears, cliffs or fire, but they also want to protect us from sources of perceived stress and distress – often the beneficial things that we actually do want, need and deserve: a job promotion, starting a new business and going after a goal that's outside our comfort zone. While these are things that won't necessarily destroy or harm us like a bear could, our brains actually don't know any better and still perceive them as threats, rallying against them with negative thoughts and emotions in an attempt to 'save' us. But there is another sinister player at work here. I want to talk to you about fear's second–in–charge (to safety): 'I'm not enough.' This is a fear that paralyses Women of Colour the most, keeps us playing small and not fulfilling our greatest potential to experience the freedom of self–actualisation, self–belief, success and social change. We end up stagnant and stuck, feeling frustrated, resentful, angry, irritable, unfulfilled and down about the world, our lives and sadly ourselves. This is the price that 'I'm not enough' makes us pay.

In early March 2019, I was working with a coach about planning for my #ColourFULL conference (a leadership and entrepreneurship conference by and for Women of Colour and allies). I was trying to set up all these meetings with prospective sponsors, doing the back-end work to set the conference up, while also working full-time and managing everything else that comes with life, and I was tired. My coach suggested the idea of a small event where I could put everyone I wanted to get on board in the same room and pitch to 30 of them at once, instead of travelling to and having 30 different meetings. Bloody brilliant, I thought. I could hit them all up in two hours and then follow up only with those who were genuinely interested. We started thinking about what it could look like and, me being me, I morphed it from a small intimate event of 30 potential sponsors with three speakers, to the official soft launch of #ColourFULL; a little taste test as to what the event could and would feel like, creating interest, energy and momentum among a community before the actual conference. The fear in my head was saying to me, 'What if only a handful of people come? The room will be empty, I'll be humiliated… everyone will see I'm stupid, that I'm not good enough.' You might wonder why I scaled up from less stressful one-on-one meetings, to a 30-person event and then to a soft launch with over 150 people and more than 10 speakers. Why make life harder, right? But the commercial part of me knew that this was the thing I needed to do to test and validate my concept and, if everything went well, generate social capital for the conference. I also really wanted to give sponsors the opportunity to experience the event; to be surrounded by Women of Colour making them (the sponsor) the 'minority' in the room, to feel and hear first-hand how much they need a conference like this. Wouldn't this be way more powerful than me sitting in their office pitching to them? I also knew that if people wouldn't pay $25 – $55 for a ticket to a soft launch evening then I needed to check my assumption that people would come to an all-day conference. I knew that I had to do this to find out for myself if the actual conference could work. I also knew that if people didn't come or if it wasn't well supported then, that was ok, at least I knew now rather than investing nearly another year of my life into it, and could move onto another idea that would work.

Humans value certainty more than happiness, and from my own past experiences and self-awareness I know that I need certainty to contain my fear. Fear largely stems from a lack of certainty (you know, all the 'what if' scenarios that usually circle around you like a shark around your head) so I use this tool called a 'Stop, Go plan' to help create that certainty and control and therefore manage my fear. It is a plan for all the likely scenarios that could occur, written down and set to a timeline with deadlines showing in green when to Go and red for when to Stop. For example, I decided that 30 people was the bare minimum I needed to see to validate the bigger idea of #ColourFULL conference. Ego-wise, 30 people was the minimum I needed to see to continue investing my time and energy into this idea. The Stop, Go plan was as follows: if 30 people had purchased tickets two weeks before the event, then I would continue with the soft launch – Go. If I had sold less than 30 tickets, then I would refund my customers and cancel the event and this was the worst that would happen – Stop. The people who did purchase a ticket or RSVP would eventually forget the would-be event and it would dissolve into the past, another idea that didn't work, joining the millions every day that don't. I am usually someone that is quick to take action on things but even with my plan I was slower to act with this one. I dabbled in it a little but still failed to take any real action. All I did was sketch out the concept and decided my Stop, Go boundary line to provide some certainty.

At the beginning of June, I was on holiday with family and reflecting about the event. A big part of me was annoyed at how I was letting my fear dictate no action on the soft launch event. I often use negative emotions as drivers for taking action so I decided to do the bare minimum but make sure that I took action in something big. I knew that if I booked something with someone external then I wouldn't retract or cancel because my fear of looking bad or letting someone down by cancelling is far stronger than my fear was of having the event and it being a big flop. It also took certainty about the event to a whole new level. The first concrete thing that needed to be done was to book the venue. I sent an email to five different venues and got one booked for the 16th of July. I picked that date as the 6th is my birthday and I consider that my lucky number. I was tempted to push the event back to August, maybe even November as I wasn't planning to have the actual conference until May the following year. But I know what I'm like and that it was really just my fear speaking – I knew I needed to follow my curiosity to end my misery and see if this was going to work. Sidenote: I want you to know that this is not a story of success after success after success. What you don't know is that prior to all this, exactly four years earlier, I had sunk to my lowest–ever point. I didn't realise until a week before the soft launch that in 2015, the 16th of July had been the very day that I had committed to changing my life after hitting rock bottom. It felt symbolic that after changing my life four years earlier, I was now empowering my sisters to change their life. The venue was booked but, still sitting in fear, I had left everything else until three weeks before the event when I had another assertive, butt–kicking conversation with myself, created a to–do list and got to work. I knew I had to give myself the chance to see if this thing could work and that I would regret it even more if I didn't take action now and cancelled, postponed or let it flop because I didn't get into gear fast enough and give it my all. The scariest tasks usually are the ones that need to be done to validate an idea and put it out there in public. For Women of Colour, this is about visibility. The scariest thing for me was to create a poster and put it up on social media with a public link to the shopping cart and see how many people purchased it. Common sense told me there was no point doing all the other items on my to–do list; all the nice, easy ticks that left me feeling safe and comfortable but didn't accomplish the real work that would validate this idea. The second task was to market it, stay focused on the process but let go of the outcome and simply observe to see the response.

I held off on the rest of my to–do list and waited to see if I would hit 30 RSVPs by the two weeks before the event. I watched as things started garnering attention. My posts were being shared and reshared, people were tagging friends and my database grew from 18 people to almost 400 in those first two weeks. A fortnight before the event, I had hit 55 tickets sold and received a heap of RSVPs from potential sponsors and stakeholders. Seven days out from the event, we were sold out and over–capacity with over 150 attending. Looking at my Stop, Go plan, these outcomes definitely meant Go! These results gave me a huge boost of confidence and energised me to start running with my to–do list, smashing it out in less than a week and leaving me time before the event to relax and tie up loose ends in a mindful way. Watching this event get sold out a week before the event was like seeing a unicorn – pure magic. I knew that it wasn't me or my brilliance but simply good–timing and my decision to choose to lean into the fear. My thoughts, feelings and actions aligned and the Universe and God answered. When the day of the event came, the room was full and buzzing with Women of Colour. The self–critical part of me was kicking myself saying, 'See! What if you had taken no action, you wouldn't have gotten to witness this!'

The day after the event, I felt overwhelmed and stressed about the responsibility and obligation I now had to the needs and wants of the more than 150 people who came, and all those that had read my posts, messaged me and joined my mailing list. I started thinking, 'What did I get myself into?' What if I can't repeat this success, let alone grow it? I can't do less; I now have to do bigger and better but what if I can't? What if it doesn't work and I fail? Now EVERYONE will know because I've geared them all up for the conference. What if I'm not enough?' I was feeling and thinking of failure before I had taken any more steps forward.

> *Fresh from the adrenaline of our success we are either addicted to the rush of self-belief and realising of potential and instantly set bigger, more ambitious and audacious goals or we crawl into a ball and retract, overwhelmed.*
>
> **#ColourFULL**

For many of us, we experience that adrenaline wearing off to be replaced by an amplification of our existing fears, or a whole new set of them. These are the emotions and thoughts that come with setting the bar higher and taking the next step; even for those goals that we say we really want. It doesn't matter what we achieve, for some it can never be enough and for most the moment is fleetingly addictive. The bigger the success, the greater the challenge the greater the potential for a higher level of fear. I don't believe we can ever eradicate fear 100% but through consistent action and by continuously stretching ourselves out into the uncomfortable, the voice and emotions of fear are softened and reduced. The less attention we give fear, the more surely our true inner-self sees and believes that it is false, and can pay less attention to it in the future. Fear is also like a muscle. The more we step into discomfort and breathe through the emotions, voices and thoughts of fear, the stronger we become; building the muscle of confidence, self-belief, self-trust and courage. The times we stay in our comfort zone and choose to give into fear, we weaken this muscle and allow levels of fear and self-doubt to increase. I was once told that the mind doesn't know the difference between good and bad and I believe this to be true when it comes to our goals that stretch us beyond our comfort zone and propel us into success versus being in a stand-off with a live bear looking at us as a snack. However, I know from past experience you can rewire the brain and train it to know that when it comes to our goals, they won't kill us, in fact it will make us stronger, turning the volume down on fear. You can practice this by continuously stepping outside your comfort zone with consistent and rigorous action. Regardless of your past achievements or failures, see that every opportunity and moment is an opportunity, a testing and training ground, to practice developing the needed 'courage muscle' that will build and create the success and future that you actually want. The power lies in your choice, not in your fear.

Tackling the tasks that fill you with fear is no different to learning a language or embarking on a new project. I encourage you to break down your goal into the smallest, most manageable step possible. Know this: action comes before motivation, not the other way around. Don't wait to feel motivated, kick your butt into action and fuel your motivation from the process and result of your actions. Positive outcomes inform your motivation, giving you evidence of your confidence, courage and self-conviction to make things happen. So, start with tiny tasks to kickstart taking action. For those that are feeling more brazen, dive into the deep end and do that one task that scares you the most. Get it out of the way because it is also likely that that one most feared task is also the most necessary to create your success and achieve your goal. By getting it done and out of the way it alleviates the pressure and makes doing the rest a total breeze. As someone who does this consistently, I can testify that nothing is as scary as we perceive it to be. And remember, if it fails it is never as bad as we imagine it to be. There is nothing scarier than remaining where you are in the next one, five or 20 years or the silent and aching pain of regret; looking back at your life as wasted years of what if and if only. By leaning into fear, you give yourself the opportunity to build the muscle of confidence, self-belief, self-trust, conviction and courage and use it to conquer fear, witnessing that the perceived threat was worse than the reality.

Your action progress framework

Start with the resources, networks or tools you have right now. Figure it out, work around it, get up, keep going, don't let up. Flex the muscle. It's the only way to keep fear at bay. Daily, consistent action. Whether they're big steps or small steps doesn't matter, it's every step that matters. Plug into your community and sisterhood for support. Keep going Sis, reframe your thoughts to those that are helpful and not harmful – believe that the world is not against you but for you. The world is ready for you and all that you have to offer. All you need to do is show up, day in day out regardless of the fear and self–doubt. When you do, you get the opportunity to see for yourself that your fear was false and you gather the evidence you need to realise that you've always been enough. This evidence puts us on the path to self–actualisation. There is nothing that helps us heal more and increase our personal power than seeing the evidence of who we truly are, our potential and witnessing the impact of that in how it transforms the world, our culture, community and future generations.

As Women of Colour, the system of oppression wants us to give into fear. It wants us to buy into these false narratives and fall into the vortex of oppression, believing that we are not enough. Every time we play small, pull back, don't show up or stay silent we affirm and validate the actions of the oppressor and give them power because at the heart of it, we are questioning our worth – just like they want us to. You choosing to stay where you are is keeping them in business but Sis, that doesn't have to be your reality. It is not mine and I know for sure, that it doesn't need to be yours. I am giving you permission to create a new narrative for yourself. Stand up, as hard as it can be sometimes, and weaken the voice of the oppressor and the system that seeks to hold us down by showing up and showing up fully as you, who you truly are. The more sisters who refuse to give into systemic discrimination and oppression, the more that feel the fear and do it anyway, the stronger we collectively become, weakening the system while empowering, giving permission and freeing other sisters to also do the same; the domino effect. A lot of the time we spend our time fighting for why our fear is justified, why it exists, why we are stuck, why we are in pain. Whatever you fight for is what you will receive and create so fight for what you do want – courage and conviction – not fear. You'll get nothing out of the first, but something magical from the second. I know it Sis, I speak from experience.

We need your talent and your special sauce. That thing that only you bring to the world. Whether it's being a mum who is present, an employee who's healed from the attacks of her manager or a CEO who has tripled net profit. The world needs you and history is replete with examples of Women of Colour who have overcome huge obstacles and stepped into the fear and beyond, creating the freedoms and successes we get to experience today – even though it is still hard and inequitable. Reach for those blueprints of your sisters past and present community to shine a light on the path and for strength, guidance, advice and support.

# #

Dig deep to take consistent daily actions, whether you 'feel like it' or not, and know that the pursuit of your purpose is worth more than giving into your limiting beliefs, fears, thoughts and emotions.

#ColourFULL

Make your action muscle stronger than your fear. Don't look at me or other people because we are not your competition, your procrastination, fear and ego are so compete against them.

# #

Success is on the other side of fear.

#ColourFULL

Remember you don't have to go at it alone; I'm here, cheering you on and walking alongside you every step of the way. You got this Sis. Remember, action is the only antidote to fear. Daily, consistent rigorous action. Action comes before motivation, before you will ever 'feel like it' (you never will) so get on with it and lean in to flex that mental muscle. If anything, fear is a sign that something incredible and transformative is about to happen, a tension of change, a breakthrough, an invitation for us to step over the bridge to claim what rightfully belongs to us. Make the life you have count. Where your focus is, your energy goes; where your energy goes is what you produce and experience. Focus on creating the life you deserve and walk through to the other side of fear to create your confidence, courage and conviction. You deserve no less.

*Share the quotes in this chapter with others
so that they too can be elevated, empowered and inspired.*

*Remember to tag Winitha so that we can reshare
your post with our global community.*
Turn to p274 for Winitha's social media handles.

6

Confidence:
it's not what you think

"The more your honor your spirit and soul, the more
that energy grows around you."

~ Lion Babe

In chapter 5, we unpacked the action progress framework: action, outcomes motivation. When I created the framework, I realised that I could do all the hypnotherapy, counselling, meditation, affirmations, reading, podcasting, motivation video watching, praying and thinking I wanted to but nothing was never going to change. I was never going to feel motivated enough to pursue X and confidence was just a dream. It wasn't until I took steps, real actions, to move beyond my fears, self–limiting beliefs and lack of motivation, regardless of how I felt or didn't feel, that my confidence levels rose. Of course, I have had many disasters that have eaten away at my confidence but when I take an action to get back up it builds my confidence in my own ability to be stronger than what I thought I was and to bounce back, set a goal and achieve it.

On the flipside it's interesting how we constantly go searching for an external source to help us feel motivated in order to feel confident to do the thing or pursue a goal. I believe motivation is a cover up for self–doubt. The root of 'I don't feel motivated' is a lack of confidence and so we create resistance and stop ourselves from doing the doing for fear that we'll be caught out as a fraud, or worse, realise that we were right and that we don't have what it takes. This is why action in the face of fear, a lack of motivation or confidence is so important. As James Clear said, every action you take is a vote for the person you want to be, the leader you already know you are deep down and the life you know you deserve. You can view confidence like a bank balance: every action we take is a deposit into our confidence reserves. When things don't work out, our balance depletes, we lose those tokens of confidence. What we must do in those moments is to take the actions to heal and rise; and when we do, we not only replace those coins but add more, leaving us more confident, anti–fragile and resilient than ever (James Clear, Atomic Habits, 2018). Confidence isn't a given personality trait nor is it something that you achieve that stays with you forever. It is something that must be cultivated by taking consistent and rigorous action. It's something that you do. Just thinking about your holiday destination is not going to take you there and confidence is no different. All the thinking, visualisation and affirmations will only take you so far. True confidence requires action so get to it, Sister.

Confidence and self-doubt: the paradoxical truth

There is a paradoxical truth to confidence. Confidence and self-doubt often travel together, fighting with one another to each take you to a different destination. It's up to you to choose which way you want to go. Life is often about holding two paradoxical truths gently in one hand. As with fear, I don't believe that we are ever truly 100% confident, we just dim the light on self-doubt and in the process turn up the light on confidence with the choices and actions we make every day, big and small – it all adds up in our confidence bank account. You can be confident and doubt yourself at the same time. And that's ok. Pay attention to the first and work on gently ignoring to release the second.

Since 2005, the year I finally committed to having a career as an entrepreneur after sitting in fear for two years, I have built and continually strengthened my confidence muscle by starting and running over seven companies, as well as a whole bunch of other 'scary' stuff. This is despite feeling unconfident, uncomfortable and a whole suite of other negative emotions. I still have self-doubt; it just doesn't debilitate and freeze me for years like it did prior to 2005. Some people see how quickly I turn out work and how quick I am to go from concept to launching it out there in the world. There are moments when I haven't been flexing my confidence muscles enough and that the voice of self-doubt gets loud, however, I am unashamed and unapologetic about the ideas I present to the world and courageous in putting them out there. I often tell people that just because I produce quickly and take loads of action, doesn't mean that there are instances where I am not screaming all the way down in the background.

As they say, courage is not the absence of fear, but rather that something is more important than the fear itself.

What I have learned is that when things don't work out or we give into self-doubt, it's because we held on to our goals too tight and didn't surrender the outcome by staying purely focused and committed to the opportunity of the process. Acknowledge, name, feel, investigate and walk through your emotions but know that life is too short to waste time sitting on the pity potty. Sometimes you need to shrug your shoulders and move on. To stay and stew in self-pity, victim mindset and internal suppression and suffering weakens confidence and puts you at risk of slipping into a big hole where, once you're in, it's hard to get out. Rather than fighting to hold on to self-doubt that holds you back, put that energy into taking consistent action to do the things that will produce results giving you confidence and rejoice that you did what only one per cent of the population does – you took action regardless of self-doubt. Celebrate that you gave it a go. It's hell of a lot more than what the other 99% of the population are choosing to do!

Shift your focus

Negative self-talk is one of the key things that inhibits us from the opportunity to build confidence. We pay way too much attention to it. A student from my LevelUP leadership and mentoring program, was mentally stuck, paying too much attention to the office politics that had been suppressing her as a Woman of Colour for over a decade. When she started working with me, she had been sucked into office politics and a toxic work culture. She had been bruised and battled by systemic discrimination, traumatised by an incident 15 years ago that had kept her back ever since. In holding onto it and every other incident that had happened since then, she was withholding her potential and voice and experiencing a whole lot of regret as a result. Even so, still in the back of her mind was this little voice that said she wanted more and so when she saw my program, she signed up in faith and hope that her current situation didn't have to be her reality for another 15 years. We got to work. In session one, she realised that although the attacks from the past weren't her fault, she had chosen to believe their narrative, telling herself that they were right and she was wrong. By holding on to these false beliefs and living in that story, she had chosen to hold herself back and as a result lost her personal power, confidence and her voice. She had deprived herself from opportunity and her leadership potential by remaining paralysed by fear. By session four her energy had shifted; energetically, she felt free. I asked her about the office politics and she said nothing had changed in that area but what had changed was her. Because of her mental shift, she didn't let their false ideas about her sink into her psyche and stay there. This shift enabled her to show up in a massive way. After practically losing her voice, she was now putting up her hand and speaking up assertively in meetings and had landed a secondment and her first speaking 'gig' at an internal event. This new action led to a profound awareness and together with the tools she had learned working with me, gave her the confidence she had so desperately wanted for all those years. In the process she attracted leadership growth opportunities. It came by shifting where her attention went and choosing confidence over self–doubt.

I repeat; 'Do the hard things and life will be easy, do the easy things and life will be hard.' The easy thing to do is to sit in self–pity and where you are the most comfortable, self–doubt. The hard thing is to shift your focus to confidence. When we choose to focus on the hurt and pain, we risk trauma attaching itself to us and manifesting into internalised suppression possibly also passing it on as intergenerational trauma. It keeps us in our comfort zone, playing small, not showing up fully and not ever reaching full potential. To be imprisoned by our pain and trauma is exactly what the oppressor and the system wants. Refuse to give in or stay in your pain and negative narratives; overcome their efforts, heal and free yourself and that of future generations. We spend so much time dwelling on why we don't have confidence and how to get it; focusing on the negative and struggling to find it. In order to change our mindset, we need to start first with actions and behaviours because they are what give us the feelings that direct our thoughts and therefore produce new neural pathways. So be aware, observe your mind and bring it back on course every time it slips towards that negative big hole. Take a detour by taking affirmative actions and behaviours that tell your inner self that you truly are confident. This will generate new feelings, ones of confidence and conviction that will direct your mind to follow.

Confidence is a learned behaviour

I heard somewhere that our parents set the baseline for what's possible; watching them live and react to life impacts how we in turn play out our own life. Whether we like it or not, they are often our first role models. Many of us also bear ancestral and intergenerational trauma, none of which we asked to take on but that has been passed down to us through our ancestors' and relatives' DNA. This is why we react to things impulsively, don't know where our instinctive emotional responses sometimes come from, or really struggle to overcome the mindsets and traits that do not serve us while still wondering why we can't just 'get over it.' We must overcome our trauma so that we don't pass this on to future generations. Ancestral, intergenerational trauma needs to end with us and healing needs to start with us. Habits, mindsets, trauma and behavioural patterns are hard wired and undoing this wiring is freaking hard. It's a lifetime journey that we need to commit to and something that we are unable to just 'get over' or 'put behind us.' The only way out is THROUGH.

Here is the truth: confidence is a learned behaviour. We can't think our way to it, we have to forge a path through action and behaviour and surround ourselves with people where this attitude is expected, the benchmark and the norm. The transformational work to heal is possible by building and learning new habits and patterns which, over time, will overshadow and hopefully override the old to become our source strength. Confidence is a choice and an action you can take every day. You will never be 100% cured of self–doubt but you will learn to pay less and less attention to it with every action you take to propel you forward to your goals and therefore towards confidence. I understand that lifetime knocks and blows to your confidence: family and cultural expectations, your lived experiences, your pain and trauma, your relationships, social conditioning, the media, racism and systemic discrimination and much more have all impacted your confidence and created a rather loud and noisy voice of self–doubt and fear (Dr Amy Silver, *The Loudest Guest*, 2020). But I'm here to tell you that you don't have to continue to accept this as your future reality. You can choose another. You have the power to set yourself free from the bondage of internalised suppression and the shackles of modern–day psychological slavery. Choose not to act on the voice of self–doubt but instead choose to act on the voice of confidence and to nurture it regardless if you are feeling it or not. Confidence is action, not a feeling. By taking action and showing regardless if you 'feel' confident or not, you'll become a straight hustler; a more confident, convicted, anti–fragile and resilient person that gives themselves permission and actively goes after what they want and know they deserve. Now THAT is confidence!

Surround yourself with confident people

Back in 2015 when I decided that I needed to change my life, one of the first things I stripped away were the relationships and people I associated with who choose to sit in victim mentality and the comfort zone of self–doubt. It was painful but over time I felt freer; I started to form new friendships with people who were obsessed with growth and development and doing deep work within themselves; action takers who were constantly working at self–conviction and confidence through their work, business and life. Being around people like this challenged and changed my own thought patterns and beliefs. When I would resort back to my pity potty, they would call me out. When I acted from a place of self–doubt, they reminded me of my inner confidence, drawing on examples in the past where I had acted and felt confident. When I made excuses, they pushed back and challenged me to do and be more and reminded me of my potential.

That said, friendship is a two–way street and one of the ways I give back to my new friends is by doing the work to raise my bar to theirs, implementing their feedback and advice and being there for them. So, when you surround yourself with people who are confident, don't just learn from them or vibe off their energy but actually dig deep, ask what worked for them, break it down into actionable steps and seek to implement those learnings.

There are confident Women of Colour all around us from high flyers on social media to CEOs, executives to our inspiring aunties, strong mothers and precious sisters. Surround yourself with people who have a little something that you want and seek to give before you get.

Growth–orientated individuals are people who want to see those around them doing the same – choosing to take action.

#ColourFULL

Rewire your mind and body

The mornings are when my 'monkey brain' comes out. I am grateful for the first 10 seconds after waking up and then BOOM – every crazy, overly dramatic, negative thought you can imagine hits me at once. Sometimes I feel the anxiety vibrating through my nervous system, particularly at moments when I am feeling stressed, tired, hormonal or overwhelmed. As someone who works for myself, if I have no meetings or appointments in the morning then I can be tempted to sleep in, falling back asleep to avoid the anxiety. What happens instead is that I subliminally stew in those thoughts and give in to the negativity and doubt, taking in this toxic energy with me throughout the day. So instead, I schedule going to the gym and because I can never bring myself to cancel last minute, I make sure that I turn up even if it means I have to drag myself there. My gym is a five-minute drive away and I set my alarm for half an hour before class, giving myself minimal time to get ready before needing to head out the door. There is literally little to no room for my monkey mind to go wild. It's not for everyone but this is the most effective way for me to get started with a positive mindset for the day. Once I'm in the gym sweating and moving, surrounded by people, I'm ok. I know I need to rigorously move my body and be around people in a high-energy environment to cut through the negative thoughts in my brain. For some, a gentler way works better; morning pages, meditation, yoga, a walk. Figure it out and do whatever works for you.

It's not a new idea, moving your body to change your state. When our brains and nervous systems are rioting, we need to short-circuit the thoughts and emotions that do not serve us and replace them with ones that do, particularly before the situation escalates and it's close to impossible to get ourselves out of the mental overwhelm. Physical action helps to break the cycle. Some of my students pull their earlobe, jump around, go for a walk or do push-ups on the spot. There are many things you can do but the key is to move your body to quieten the voice self-doubt and amp up the voice of confidence.

Do it to be it

Our confidence lies in our actions, not just our thoughts. As mentioned, the paradoxical truth is that self–doubt and confidence dwell side by side. Every time we take positive action, we prove to ourselves that we are not a self–doubter doing the easy things or giving into fear, but instead someone taking action and doing the thing that a confident person would do – the 'hard stuff.' This is the evidence your brain needs to see to build confidence. Without regular practice to reinforce and strengthen the foundation, this pattern will unravel itself. The key is not the depth or width of the action but in the consistency. So, break down the steps: if you want to be a speaker, you don't need to speak to an audience of one thousand people, you just need to have one conversation with a stranger every week, or do a Facebook Live every day. Then, with every confidence 'token' you gain with each action you take, you'll soon be reaching out to speak in front at a 1,000–person event. Confidence requires consistent, rigorous, deliberate practice, the undertaking of action regardless of fear or its existence. Consistent action build confidence and reinforces the realisation that when you do step into fear, something amazing is on the other side – not something scary. This belief softens any assumptions we have for worst–case scenarios and allows us the opportunity to see for ourselves that they are no scary monsters in the closet.

It starts with baby steps. Break it down into the smallest possible action and do that first, consistently every day. Momentum and consistency are your golden ticket to confidence.

Ritual, leverage and momentum

Leverage the times you lean into and feel confidence to fuel further confident actions. This will create, sustain and accelerate momentum to create success and achieve your leadership goals. Leverage those moments by staying plugged in and stretching yourself just a little bit to push your baseline and find your potential. It's always the last few reps in an exercise, when your muscle is the most fatigued, that you build strength and muscle (anti–fragility). Clever people leverage moments to create more success and confidence; they don't settle.

Some of us use celebration as energy to create momentum to do the next thing. It's important to celebrate your achievements and create a ritual around it. Whether it is having a dinner party or treating yourself to something. One of the things I get my students to do is to write a 'love note' to themselves and to their accountability buddy telling themselves how proud they are, giving themselves plenty of adoration and praise. I also encourage them to record all of their achievements since their first childhood memory to now and to count them up. When you are presented with this information, look yourself squarely in the eyes in the mirror and ask, 'Does this information inform me that I am 'stupid,' 'not smart enough,' 'not good enough' and 'not confident?' Or does it tell me that I have confidence? That I am indeed strong, anti–fragile, resilient and confident; that if I could overcome and achieve all that then I can do the thing I am fearing the most right now. That I am indeed confident.' Keep track of all your achievements: every thank you note or emails of praise from clients, stakeholders, managers and store them in a 'celebrate–me' document. Track your achievements at work and quantify them as if you were going to produce a report on yourself. For those of you who are visual, do a celebration–board; stick up those testimonials, emails and texts of praise as well as anything else that symbolises your achievements and look at this daily, reflect and ponder on it conjuring feelings of self–admiration and confidence. These are the stripes that you have earned. No one else did. Viewing this evidence daily just before you awaken or slumber will give your confidence a boost and sustain it consciously, unconsciously and subconsciously.

To procrastinate is to resist doing what you need to do to change your life, the real work. Resistance is the child of fear and self–doubt so lean into and embrace resistance because it is pointing towards the exact thing that is needed to build and strengthen your confidence muscle. The denial of self can paralyse us, keep us captive to self–doubt and immobilise us in taking action. You are more in control of your life and your existence than you think. To build psychological, emotional, intellectual and spiritual fitness, to build confidence, shift your focus and accept that you are deserving of achieving everything that you desire. Take small actions every day; set a goal, break it down into teeny steps and take one step today and do everything you can in your power to maintain consistency and momentum, then leverage it. You got this, Sis. Confidence is built through action, something that you do, not something that you feel. It's behaviour and repeated action that builds new neural pathways, mindsets, belief and feelings and thoughts of confidence. Build the necessary evidence your mind and body need to see right now to cultivate and nurture self–belief. The feelings will come, just gently ask the ones that are no longer serving you to move aside so you can focus on confidence and take action. And as for action, well that's simply a choice. Deposit those confidence tokens into your bank balance and put in votes for the type of person you know you are deep down inside and the leadership journey and life you deserve. You are a confident and incredible Woman of Colour.

I'm here rooting for you, loving you and supporting you from the background. You are confident, accept that fact and bring your true confident self to the surface to unleash that powerful, clever and brilliant you onto your dreams, goals and the world unapologetically and unashamedly! You are a confident leader so take action right now. Life's short, make the one you have today count.

Share the quotes in this chapter with others
so that they too can be elevated, empowered and inspired.

Remember to tag Winitha so that we can reshare
your post with our global community.
Turn to p274 for Winitha's social media handles.

7

Motivation:
fire, aim, ready

"I raise up my voice – not so that I can shout, but so that those without a voice can be heard...we cannot all succeed when half of us are held back."

~ Malala Yousafzai

As Women of Colour, I can understand why many of us don't feel motivated. We may have had the juice punched out of us due to idiotic people in our career that have discriminated against us; we may be caretakers, taking care of just about everyone and their dog. Even the office housework gets thrown our way. Some of us have little support from community and family around, people who can babysit the kids if need be, be an ear to listen to, support us, introduce us to potential opportunities and people who can open doors. Constant striving and hardship dim the lights on motivation and, for some of us, the electricity has been cut off completely. I write this feeling quite unmotivated. One half of my brain is saying, 'Yay, we are writing' while the other side says, 'I can't be bothered – can we watch a movie already?' You can be doing what you always dreamed of doing and still feel unmotivated; doing what you say is your calling and passion and still be unmotivated. For me, since I was 15, this was to start a business and work for myself. Now I am finally doing it and I want to watch a movie?! 'Seriously, Winitha – the world needs the gift of the calling you have been given so get over yourself and just freaking WRITE' is what I told myself. And so here we are, ironically, on the chapter about motivation. So that's what I'm doing today; I'm staying in motion, staying plugged in. I'm staying on course and flexing that muscle, committing to seating my fine, brown arse down to spend three hours writing this chapter and it does not get up to prance around until it's done.

Stay in motion and stay in the game, Sister. It's consistency over quantity or quality; build the muscle that creates a habit loop and keep those habits and others strong and sustainable. Show up every day and even if it's one step or one action make sure it's meaningful and intentional. It's the key to staying motivated.

# #

You are our future. The world needs us and our leadership.

#ColourFULL

Remember motivation requires evidence and results and this only comes as outcomes from your action not by 'feeling motivated.' Sister, you are in good hands. I have motivation issues in truckloads and this is what makes me qualified on the subject. I've experienced traditional forms of feeling unmotivated such as procrastination and resistance and non–traditional forms like the kind that is lurking in the closets of many so–called busy–bees.

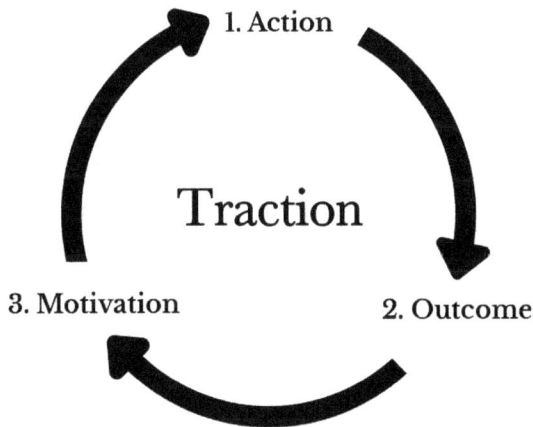

1. Action

Traction

3. Motivation   2. Outcome

Your action progress framework

At around six years old, I was a budding artist. I had forced my parents to buy me oil paints, these tiny little canvases and cheap paint brushes. I was fully convinced that I had the ability to win the Archibald prize, Australia's most prestigious and coveted art competition. So, I took lots of action, sketching every day and never went on a car ride without packing my teddy bear backpack with a sketchbook and pencils. I had read in the Australian Artist Magazine and books that real artists capture everything they see and are constantly practicing and so at this young age I developed the ability to stay extremely organised and project manage myself. I created a schedule for every day of the summer school holidays, blocking in developmental stages and start and end dates for the paintings I was going to work on. I was busy with all the fluff, dancing around the edges without firming up on my commitment to myself. What I really needed to do to achieve my dream was to boldly ask my parents for art classes where I could get expert criticism and advice. I needed to visit art galleries, participate in art competitions and get my artwork out there. A tall feat for any six–year–old but you get my drift.

As humans, we can have severe self–esteem issues and still be the most selfish, egotistical and superficial person out there; we are motivated when we see results. We feed our ego with the desire to feel and show that we are busy (#hustling) and receive immediate results and a quick high by ticking meaningless tasks off a list. For those who have a business it's stuff like fluffing over business cards, branding, logos or working on version five of their website. We get caught up in this busy–work instead of drafting the concept, getting it 'good enough' and hitting the marketing and sales like our life depended on it. It's much scarier to put you and your idea out there asking people to buy your product than to create a Facebook page or obsess over a website. For those in a job, it's busy–work IN the job as opposed to strategically working ON the leadership journey. Constant busyness gets us nowhere, we throw our hands up in the air and dramatically declare we are unmotivated and burn out, leading us to eventually give up on the thing we said we wanted and declaring it and ourselves a failure. Doing the fluffy stuff may get you some teeny–weeny results through luck or from compounded effort over a long duration of time but unless you do the thing you are avoiding right now, that you know you is the number–one thing you need to be doing to move you furthest towards your goal, you won't see the real results that are going to get you truly motivated to take the next step. In fact, you will see little to no return on the investment of your time and energy, which you will never get back, on fruitless and meaningless tasks. When we constantly 'busy' ourselves around the edges and avoid the real, deep, difficult, often uncomfortable and intentional work it's no wonder we get demotivated. We are not doing the work that is going to get us the kind of results we are really looking for, that is going to give us real meaning and value through its impact. After wasting so much time and energy on actions that bear no fruit or outcomes and getting nothing back in return, we are bound to get demotivated. And in my experience and my research of many successful Women of Colour leaders before me, it has been the challenging and uncomfortable work that gets real results – not the superficial or day-to-day stuff.

In his book *The ONE Thing*, Gary Keller states that there are people in the word who can work just as hard as you or even more intensely for longer hours. The indicator of success is not how long or how intensely you work but which actions you choose to work on (Gary Keller, *The ONE Thing*, 2012). I know this to be true from my own experience. When I was working a corporate job, I used the same process to work on my leadership and business goals. I am obsessed with ticking off goals, not to-do lists. Every week now, I take a few hours on a Sunday to implement a framework and process that has been intensely and ruthlessly pared down to only doing the tasks that will take me the furthest towards my goals. I then schedule these into my diary with the most important tasks (those that have the most impact and will drive me the furthest towards achieving my goal) getting priority and the rest including the day-to-day stuff fitting in around them. As my students in my LevelUP program know, what gets scheduled in gets done (not what gets added to the to-do list let alone written down in some arbitrary notebook). What truly makes us motivated is when we can clearly see and feel ourself making traction, growing and moving closer towards achieving a goal. True, sustainable motivation is created when we first take meaningful, deeply intentional and strategic action towards our goals. It's traction that creates motivation and, like confidence, motivation isn't something you get by thinking or feeling alone. It's something that you do. It's action.

Some of us fall into the honeymoon–phase trap. We see this usually at the start of the calendar year when people get super excited about their goals and how they are going to change their life. Eventually the honeymoon ends and reality sits in. The journey towards achieving a goal is in the process and no process is simple. All of us want to hide under the bedcovers sometimes, I bet even Michelle Obama does, but she shows up anyway. Even during the height of her and Barack's political career, when the media would constantly target her to try and pull her down for what she wore to what she said, she still showed up day in day out, strategically and intentionally. So to you I say (with love), Sis, get over yourself. This isn't about you, this is about the impact and influence you are going to have on those that desperately need it, and being of service to others from a place of personal power and healing. It's about freeing yourself so you can give permission to other Women of Colour and future generations to also do the same and to leave a legacy, a blueprint and trodden path for them to follow and widen for other Women of Colour. The world needs the gifts and talents you were created and purposed for to transform it with your exceptional and inspiring leadership. You're not alone, your ancestors, community, sisters and I are with you every step of the way. We've got your back. So, move on and get on with it. You've got work to do Sis!

Building motivation

The first few steps towards your goals that build a sense of motivation will feel like when you start pedalling a bicycle. The first few pushes are hard, then we get a bit of momentum and pace and it gets easier. It is in the first few pushes of the pedals that most people give up or come to a complete stop. And for others, when it gets easy and they get some pace up is when they get comfortable and complacent, stop pedalling and fall off without reaching their destination. Stay in motion to maintain your pace, reach your goal and stay motivated. Staying in the process and staying in motion is easier than coasting, stopping and then having to start again from the beginning. It's easy to stop, it's not easy to start. Stay in motion. As the first few pushes are what takes a lot of effort and action, I recommend that you sprint your way through this initial phase. If we take our time, we allow room for fear, excuses and justifications to creep in and sabotage our progress and commitment. Sprinting also demands that we back ourselves, building the muscle and skill to stay focused. The brain will always default to what is most familiar. Use the focus of the sprint to unearth and push through the limiting beliefs, fear, negative emotions and a truckload of self–doubt and replace them with a mindset filled with self–love, self–compassion and self–belief. Keep this mentality for those hill–climbs that will also challenge you. In those moments there is no room for self–doubt which will only have you sliding down to and staying at the bottom of a valley. Staying in motion and keeping momentum is what makes the journey easier, not harder. Momentum is like the wind you need behind your back, supporting you to keep your pace and reach your destination.

Sprint to push through internal barriers and create momentum

Get sprinting

Any successful person will tell you that there is no magic elixir to motivation. It takes good old action, the kind of action that is going to get you results and the kind of action that is most likely going to make you feel uncomfortable, stretched and very unmotivated. And you know what? No one promised you it would be easy, but I do promise that it will be worth it. Expecting to be motivated enough to take action is kind of like expecting to win the lottery without buying a ticket first. Every day we are surrounded by tasks that we don't feel motivated by; they can be chaotic, and difficult or plain boring but they are necessary if we want to achieve our leadership, career, business and life goals.

> *It's the small actions that produce the small wins that kick start our motivation to strive for the bigger.*
>
> *#ColourFULL*

Yes, the feeling of motivation is important but it's not the most important thing. Taking the action to buy a lottery ticket is.

Here are some guiding principles and meaningful actions that I hope will challenge your view on motivation and give you clarity around how to get started.

People help those who help themselves first: stay in motion

Actions will always speak louder than words. When we start aligning out actions to our words, we attract opportunities, people, resources. Merely talking is not enough and just because it has worked for men and White people doesn't mean that we, as Women of Colour should follow suit. Instead, we can create and set a new trend, live a life of integrity and take actions that align and back our words, values, beliefs, goals and dreams. The people who do this are rare and it will make you stand out by a mile. Living a life of integrity is worth more than all the success in the world. People help people who are able to help themselves first. People are attracted to people that have a momentum gathering around them through the action they are taking. People want to be a part of that energy. They want to help people make dreams come true when they see traction; they want to be a part of the journey. Words don't stick or create a legacy but actions do, so ensure your actions speak louder than your words and over time you'll attract success your way, giving you the motivation to turn up the volume another notch and leave a legacy. Your actions are your testimony to who you are.

We often pray to a God but the truth is that God can't help us if we are stagnant. Just like people, God requires us to get into motion and meet them halfway. When we are in motion, we demonstrate that we are going to do something with whatever it is God has given us. Being in motion also takes us away from the self-centredness and ego that comes with sitting on the pity potty. So, if you're praying hard or putting intentions out to the Universe or God for motivation, a revelation, confirmation or a dream, first take a few steps towards it and keep showing up day in day out and week after week, working what you have like it's the only thing you got. Even when God or the Universe doesn't show up, you do. Keep the wheels in motion, surrender to a higher being and keep focused on the bigger picture. God rewards those that are able to help themselves first. God propels those forward and creates momentum for those that are already in motion and have demonstrated commitment to work in line with their desires. Stop waiting and expecting God to part the seas and do all the hard work. God is not a fairy godmother. Get into motion regardless of whether you feel motivated or not and the Universe will reward you by meeting you halfway.

The clock is ticking

When I was 16 years old, I lost a close friend of mine and it forever changed my view of the world. She didn't get a second chance but I still had mine. The older I've gotten, the more I've started losing other friends to cancer, suicide, accidents. It has made me look at what I am choosing to do with my own life and honour their lives by living mine, mistakes, failures and all. Humans are a weird bunch of people. Some of us need terrible loss or pain to kick us into gear after hitting rock bottom. Others live life as though they are under a constant anaesthetic while some float through life until a traumatic life–changing moment shakes them up. We treat life and every moment of it as if we are going to live on indefinitely. But should we really let it get to that? Every minute that passes is a minute lost and a minute that has taken you closer to your expiry date. Remember, you get to determine the course of your life. You are not a helpless creature. You have the ability to do anything if you choose to at any age and any moment. As annoyingly easy as that sounds this is the absolute truth. And every time you step into this new paradigm, you give permission for another Woman of Colour to do the same! Life is short, make the one you have right now count. Don't wait to feel motivated. Get cracking!

You'll get over it but first get on with it

The fear that grips you feels real and I believe it's important to name and be aware of our emotions. Yet I also feel that we have a natural tendency to turn ourselves towards negativity that allows us to justify all the rationalising that's in our heads about our inaction. The media has an overwhelming overemphasis on failure which poo–poos all over our motivation. When I post negative content, I get plenty of reactions on social media but when I post something positive that could genuinely move the needle forward in people's lives, hardly anyone engages. As humans we are attracted to drama, regardless of whether that drama exists inside our head or on Instagram. Everyone wants to spend their time and energy talking about what's not working and yet no one seems to have any clue, or the time and energy, to create solutions and focus on what will work.

It's easy to talk about what's not working.
It's hard to come up with a solution.

#ColourFULL

Yes, it's important to talk about what's not working, it's necessary for collective, ancestral and individual healing, freedom and self–expression but staying there is when it gets problematic. As I've said before, staying in the problem is like being circled by a great white shark. Eventually the only thing we risk is ourselves and our very lives. Don't stay stuck on all the negative content, people to blame, shame, excuses, justifications, why the world is full of idiots or if Donald Trump's hair is real or not. Get on with getting on. Move forward, stay in motion.

Use your competitive streak

If you are like me, one of the things that might get you going is competition. When I was hesitating about putting together the soft launch of #ColourFULL, I met up with some Women of Colour who said they wanted to support the conference but I quickly realised that they actually wanted to do something very similar and were picking my brain. Within the space of two weeks, they got cracking pretty quick, which gave me the kick up the bum I needed – competition and FOMO (fear of missing out). Now, collaboration over competition is my motto and I did genuinely want to see them succeed and gave them my support but I also leveraged my competitive gene to get me into gear. In the end, they lost momentum after a month and gave up as I raced to the finish line. Some of us will feel intimidated and give up and others don't like to leverage negative emotions but competition gets me out of a funk pretty quickly and ignites my action gene. Now when I feel FOMO, I check myself into action and leverage it to accelerate. Not all negative emotions are bad for us; I leveraged my competitive gene to continue to grow and excel in my career. Use your competitive spirit to ignite your butt into action and get you into motion regardless if you feel motivated or not.

Raise the stakes so it hurts

Sometimes the investment of time and energy is not enough to kick us into action – that's when we need to raise the stakes. For some people this is selling their house, investing in a venture and couch surfing until they make it or quitting their job so they have no choice but to make their business work. For others it's putting their hand up to present at a meeting and be seen in front of executives or sitting at the front of a live event. The key with raising the stakes is to raise them to a point where it 'hurts' to cause some pain or tension (but not overwhelmingly). To raise the stakes means to increase the investment and therefore the risk, so that if you lost, it would be substantial.

Here are 10 ways you can raise the stakes to propel you into action when you are not feeling motivated:

1. Give someone you respect and trust half of your savings and tell them to give it to you back when you've achieved your goal.

2. Put it out there in the world publicly and leverage the negative emotion that comes with not doing/achieving it – saving face.

3. Refuse to watch that movie you've been desperately wanting to watch till you complete a certain task. Have your fun 'funded' when you have achieved your goal.

4. Unsubscribe to Netflix, Amazon Prime, Stan and whatever else including social media on all your devices until you complete a certain task or give your laptop, TV or mobile to a friend until you complete what you need to.

5. Make a declarative statement on social media and ask people to hold you accountable. Post updates daily or get an accountability buddy.

6. Book yourself into a pricey hotel or go to a friend or relative's place and refuse to go home until you've completed something. Make a pact with your friend or relative that you are not to go home until you can show them that you've got the work done.

7. Choose the expensive course or coach that stretches your budget. Cheaper courses and professionals/coaches don't stretch us financially and create the needed incentive/tension to really milk the opportunity and do the work.

8. Take a sabbatical or leave without pay from your job for a set duration of time to give yourself a deadline and financial pressure to tick off your goals but also a safety net if it doesn't work out.

9. Join a mastermind/accountability group whose bar is higher than yours. The energy of the accountability group will be contagious and over time you will want to raise your bar to reach theirs.

10. Set your tasks for the day and then commit to doing the one task that you least want to do or that you fear the most. Get it out of the way to give yourself the motivation to bulldoze the other items in your to–do list. Alternatively, get a few quick wins under your belt to gain the momentum you need to address other, bigger items. Whatever works for you.

Prime your mind

In the mornings, I exercise, meditate, shower, pray out loud, eat breakfast and then future script. During this time, I don't check my emails and my phone stays in my kitchen drawer on silent and my laptop in my office, both are out of sight. This process of future scripting positions me to get focused and take action, visualising and feeling the emotions of the goal I am currently pursuing and giving me the needed feel–good hormone hits to want to take action. It keeps me focused on the bigger picture, not stuck down in all the chaos in my head and aligns my feelings to my thoughts and actions (hello Law of Attraction!). Before I go to bed, I do another round of future scripting to prime my mind for the next day, view my diary for the next and visualise myself smashing it and enjoying every part of it as well as the moments when my goals and dreams are achieved.

\#

What gets scheduled in gets done, not what is written down, visualised only, thought about in my head or put on a to–do list or notebook

#ColourFULL

Get organised and create the right environment

Those that know me very well, know that I maintain a colour–coded scheduled diary seven days a week. Everything gets scheduled in: when I sleep, wake, shower, travel time, grocery shopping, talk to friends on the phone, housework etc. The only thing that doesn't get scheduled in are moments of surprise like when I need to pee!

Break tasks down into the smallest task you can do and prioritise them in terms which will get you the most traction/value towards achieving your goal. Get clarity on what goals and tasks will drive you the farthest and quickest to achieving your purpose as opposed to what you 'feel' like doing. Prioritise and take the first few tasks, estimate how long it will take you to complete them and schedule them into your diary. Being organised is key, all you need to do now is follow your schedule.

Set yourself up for success and create an inspiring workspace in your home. Think about all the things external to you that put you in the mood to work. Set up your environment so that it is inviting, positive, comfortable and is one you want to work in. I have my headphones on with upbeat music playing in the background. I know that I get glum and unmotivated when I can't see outside so my desk at home faces the window that gets the afternoon sun and in the evening I can see the Moon. My home office is warm, cosy and uncluttered.

Create a crisis management plan

There are and will be times when you want to give up and that's usually just before we are about to achieve our goal and achieve breakthrough. Post your crisis plan somewhere visible and accessible: a little card in your wallet or screensaver on your phone for those times where you want to give up and or don't feel like it, somewhere accessible. Make it three to five steps to get you back on track and take action. For me, it's getting outside my head straight away and calling a friend; I have a list of three and if none are available,

I send them a desperate text and move on to item two. Like childbirth, even though we are exhausted, perhaps in pain and think we can't do it anymore, this is the exact moment when we are almost there to giving birth to our dream, we need to muster everything we got and give a few last big pushes. Create a plan of effective tools and strategies you can engage to get you back into the game in those moments when you may not be able to think clearly. Call a trusted friend who is your number–one cheerleader, move your body or even take a break to hit reset for a predefined period of time and get back into the game the next day; taking time off with a commitment to getting back to it in 24 – 48 hours can ease the tension and keep you on track, clearing your head and giving you space to maintain focus. Lastly, remind yourself why you are doing this and that you deserve to give yourself the opportunity to try.

Decide on your non–negotiables

We need to stay energised. It's easy to get confused between energy and motivation. We need a balance of spiritual, emotional, social, financial, intellectual, physical, environmental and sexual energy. When students in my LevelUP program feel 'unmotivated' to go after their dream or goal I ask them the question, 'What's lacking in your life right now? What are you craving right now?' The answer generally points in the direction of one of the energy–fuel tanks that is running on empty. To avoid getting to that place where you experience burnout, give yourself permission to reach for those things, put in place your non–negotiables for all energy areas and ensure it is scheduled so that it gets done. For me, gym, church, prayer time, affirmation and journaling time, 'me time,' social outings, cleaning my house, seeing my little nephew, check–ins with my psychologist and nutritionists are some of my non–negotiables. I schedule them into my electronic diary as recurring items so I don't need to think about it week–to–week. Everything else in life, including the unexpected, works around it. These are things that don't get moved, rescheduled or deleted for anyone (including myself) or anything. Everything and everyone comes after it. They are my non-negotiables.

Get an accountability buddy

An accountability buddy is a great asset. Someone with a like-minded goal who you can do daily or weekly check-ins (a quick rundown on what you plan to get done) and checkouts with (what actually happened that week), share notes and hold each other accountable to your plans, cheering us on when we feel unmotivated. Choose wisely.

Make a game of it

Timers and 'beat the clock' games really work for me to get stuff done and I've been using this tool from early on in my career. For example, I knew that I needed to differentiate myself in the job market and that employers valued productivity. When I worked in Canada, I had this boss, a Vice President (VP) that reported to the CEO who I was already hella scared of, tell me that 'Aussies are lazy' and that just keeping up with her would not be sufficient, that I needed to be two steps ahead of her at all times. For me in my early 20s, this was rather daunting. She worked 16 hour-days, seven days a week and was way more experienced and skilled than I was. I thought, 'Well, if I am going to be two steps ahead of you then shouldn't I be the VP?' After crying in the bathroom for 2 hours I decided to make a game out of it, seeing if I could anticipate the next two, even four moves ahead of her, and viewed the daily work like a chess game to see if I could outdo her. And I did, so much so that she put me, her sidekick (Executive Officer), in charge when she went away instead of one of the executive directors. When I left the organisation, the ice queen threw me a surprise goodbye party; this really showed me that I could do the impossible and outdo even someone like her and she knew it!

The process was never meant to be all fun all the time. We are imperfect people living in an imperfect world. Let go and surrender your attachment to motivation. Stay laser focused on your career, business and life goals. Take action before you're ready and the motivation will show up organically; it's an output, a by–product of the process. Stay in action and stay in motion to get and stay motivated.

Share the quotes in this chapter with others
so that they too can be elevated, empowered and inspired.

Remember to tag Winitha so that we can reshare
your post with our global community.
Turn to p274 for Winitha's social media handles.

8

Move the needle:
on your inner world

"Greatness is not measured by what a [person] accomplishes, but by the opposition [they have] overcome to reach [their] goals."

~ Dorothy Height

As Women of Colour, when we take control of our own narrative and trajectory, we start to create a different kind of freedom for ourselves, our sisters and future generations. Through our collective success and leadership, every generation chips away and weakens the oppressor and their efforts; every action and decision we take counts in the fight against systemic discrimination and racism and the quest for freedom. History offers a wealth of examples of Women of Colour who experienced severe oppression and succeeded on their terms such as Amina of Zaria, Rani of Jhansi, Elizabeth Marie 'Betty' Tallchief and Madam C. J. Walker. Our ancestors are a testimony of our ability to go forth in the face of suppression and oppression. They fought hard for the few liberties we have today and paved a way forward for us. We are everything they hoped, believed and dreamed for, everything they fought and worked for. Their revolutionary blood is the same that pumps through your veins. If our ancestors could do it so can you; to charge forth courageously honours their legacy and forges a path for future generations.

In order to advance in your career and become a powerful leader that transforms the world, the first thing we need to do is to move the needle on our inner world. Think of your leadership journey like a new fitness regimen; in order to limit the number of potential injuries (resilience) and come out stronger (anti–fragility), we need to do a little prep before we begin, during and after. Preparation is key to ensuring peak performance. To prepare we follow a strict nutrition plan, warm up before and cool down after workouts to prevent injuries, condition and strengthen muscles to get stronger, leaner and perform better and also frame the mindset needed to push and extend peak performance beyond what we perceive is possible. Then there's the massage and physiotherapy to support the process and keep you in consistent motion, and the list goes on. When we engage in this level of preparation, we get so much more out of our efforts and thrive long–term compared to someone who just turned up and started working out with no real preparation, no plan, no warmup, no goals and no support. See the difference there; the level of effort, time and strategy spent on the preparation (their inner world) versus the actual work (their outer world) to ensure that their efforts produce maximum rewards? This is the difference between amateurs and professionals, as pointed out by author Steven Pressfield. Becoming a leader is not as simple as just applying for that job or promotion and telling your boss you want to be a leader. 80% of the work to attain goals is in the preparation and the process. The preparation will give you a solid foundation to succeed from and ensure that the time spent in the process is effective and efficient, supporting you to create sustainable and long–term exponential success.

If being silent is being part of the problem, not taking action is as well.

#ColourFULL

Silence isn't just a lack of words, it's also a lack of affirmative action. Don't be overwhelmed by it, simply do what you have the energy and time for right now, be consistent and you will find your rhythm. Take strategic and calculated actions. Back and activate your faith and your words with your actions. These three elements are a powerful trio and will make up part of your armour and toolkit to success and leadership. You have everything you need inside of you: the talent, skills, cultural and ancestral wisdom and knowledge and expertise required to advance. Now all you need are a few extra tools that successful Women of Colour have used to become leaders, effectively 'beat the system' and prove its falsehoods. The system and its oppressors want you to believe that you are powerless, to be fearful and intimidated, feeling that you will never overcome it so that you don't fully show up let alone try. When the truth of the matter is that they in fact fear us and our power, which is why they oppress. When a person is threatened, they attack. Our prep game, efforts and success are our warfare and activism, the little rattles and shakes we create which weaken the system with every Woman of Colour leader that rises up. Time spent cultivating and nurturing your prep game leads to more output for your time and energy. Create a game plan and execute it masterfully. Commit to being the master of your career, a professional and not an amateur. To move the needle on your external world (your career and leadership journey), you must first move the needle on your internal world (your inner fitness; you). Sis, it's time to level up your prep game.

Here are the foundational elements that will maintain, build and move the needle on your inner world – necessary tools in your game plan, preparation and tool kit; your armoury as you venture out to achieve success and leadership.

Self-acceptance and love

The poet Audre Lorde said that self-care is political warfare. This reflects my key message that regardless of what may come our way as Women of Colour, when we choose to rise and experience internal freedom as success, we are refusing to submit to the attacks of the oppressor and are instead fighting back. This is itself an act of political warfare but one grounded in self-acceptance, compassion, care and love. Self-acceptance and self-love don't give us permission to be terrible human beings. Self-acceptance means accepting yourself wholly as you are, flaws and all, and working on the parts of you that no longer serve you or others through rigorous honesty and being a good human. It means doing the work to nurture, sharpen and develop all aspects of yourself that will support you now and into the future.

Taking the time and action to ensure that we make amends and heal so that we are supporting ourselves, not self-sabotaging and are in a position to support our sisters and communities. Being overly self-critical is not self-love or acceptance and, rather than taking that path, we need to focus on self-love and compassion. Self-love is a choice to turn down the dial on self-criticism, believing in yourself and your capacity to make your dream and goals come true regardless of external suppression and oppression and creating space and opportunities for other Women of Colour. It's setting and maintaining boundaries and creating time and energy to go for what we know we want, need and deserve. Unashamedly.

Faith and belief

Regardless of your spiritual beliefs, believing that what you want is possible is pivotal to achieving it. Many of us have lost faith because of trauma, hardship and the ordeals that we have endured as Women of Colour. We have lost faith in the ability of a higher power to provide, in ourselves and the world. Faith is a choice that we can make regardless of our current circumstances and emotions; by choosing faith we choose not to remain suppressed. We revolt against the narratives they try to force on us to believe. We choose to have faith in ourselves, in a higher power's ability to move us forward, and faith to make the seemingly impossible possible. Faith is a practice, something that needs to be engaged with consistently, even when things are going swell.

Words matter

What we say and think is what we attract and bring into our life. Words ingrain patterns of thinking, habits and beliefs into our conscious, unconscious and subconscious mind. The emotions we feel are based on this wiring in our brain and we act on those thoughts, beliefs, habits and emotions. Even though it might be your reality doesn't mean you need to voice it, feed it or buy into it. Remember my story from chapter two about my struggle to learn dance choreography? I kept telling myself I was forgetful and that I had a terrible memory; I was giving in to these negative emotions and reinforcing the wiring in my brain that I had a memory problem. It took a while but after letting the feelings of humiliation, self–doubt and shame drift past, I stayed committed, battled my inner self like you wouldn't believe, replaced my thoughts and words with positive ones and worked my arse off. You can do this too.

Starting now is better than never.

#ColourFULL

The way we have been thinking and talking has created some pretty strong neural pathways in our brains but that doesn't mean that we can't alter them. It takes lots of hard work and absolute commitment – it's a life long journey. In times of stress and frustration your mind will be tempted to default to familiar, old patterns of thinking that it used for years but that's ok because if you persist these defaults will become fewer and less frequent. When it does happen, pick yourself up from where you left off and keep going, keep persisting. The mind is more powerful than you think so use its potential to propel your career forward not hold you back.

Physical health

You cannot perform at your peak mental performance if your physical health is in bad shape. Physical strength and health make you feel on top of your game, giving you the stamina to endure long days to keep focus. Prevention is better than cure; stay on top of it to stay on top. I rarely get sick and I put this down to the fact that I eat loads of fresh vegetables and exercise at least five times a week. On my rest days, I go for a brisk walk, do stretches or get a massage to keep up my commitment to my physical health and stay on the bandwagon. You only get one body and taking care of it is your responsibility. There is no excuse or justification. Commit to taking action to nurture your physical health so that your body and mind can support you in your journey towards creating success for yourself, your family, your sisters and your community. Nurture it now, don't wait to be motivated. Doing your part to stay as physically healthy and strong as you can is your activism and part of how you will reclaim your power. Life wasn't meant to be done alone so surround yourself with other sisters who also treat their body like the goddess it is, prioritising and making an absolute commitment to their physical health and strength. We are stronger together, literally!

Emotional and spiritual resilience

These aspects of resilience are a little tricky. There is a fine line between what demands our attention and inner work and what needs professional psychological or psychiatric support. Sometimes it is hardship that gives us the tension needed to create resilience. I reframe hardships and challenges as training grounds; opportunities for me to flex and build my spiritual and emotional resilience muscle by feeling the emotions that arise with those experiences and moving through them, even when they morph into a rollercoaster. For those who don't believe in God, I suggest that you seek your spiritual resilience from within yourself. My spiritual practice saved me after I hit rock bottom, I had no choice but to reach and cling to a power higher than myself to lift me from falling into a bottomless giant hole. I have spent a lot of time and energy cultivating my spiritual beliefs, foundations and resilience. My bounce–back rate from perceived failure is faster now and those situations don't cut deep as they would have in the past, let alone hold me back.

To build emotional resilience I am a strong advocate of speaking to registered psychologists and counsellors. I recommend connecting with mental health professionals who are Women of Colour as they have a firmer understanding of what we go through and give us that safe space to fully open up and discuss past trauma. I and many other Women of Colour I speak to struggle with internalised suppression. We find ourselves instantly triggered by things to the point where it sets us back significantly and we struggle to get back up. When we lash out as a triggered response to discriminatory behaviour we encounter, we risk jeopardising the psychological and cultural safety of others, retraumatising ourselves and affirm and fuel the efforts of the oppressor. Our suffering is exactly what they want to see. This internalised suppression shows up in any number of ways: living from a place of excuses and justifications, engaging in lateral violence and discriminatory behaviour towards our sisters and people from our own or other ethnic communities, or deliberately shutting the door of opportunity on our own sisters thinking that there is only one seat at the table. When we compete instead of collaborate with our fellow sisters, we suppress, oppress, sabotage and hold them down in their careers for our own gain. The unfortunate reality and truth are that when we engage in this behaviour, we are actually further suppressing ourselves and sabotaging our own leadership efforts; divide to conquer is the strategy of the oppressor. These examples sadden my heart that we aren't dealing with our own internalised suppression by prioritising our own healing. In my work I choose to do the exact opposite of that. I want to bring us together to have each other's backs, advocate for each other, understand and leverage on the strengths of each other and stand in solidarity, collectively raising ourselves up and strengthening us as a community as we forge forward in our revolution.

#

> *It is our responsibility to take care of our internalised suppression and trauma for the psychological and cultural safety of each other so that we thrive collectively as a community. This is what it means to truly stand in solidarity. True leadership is an inside job and requires us to do deep work from the inside out.*
>
> **#ColourFULL**

As our success grows, so too do the challenges. As you step into leadership, your status and visibility increase and you may experience more outright and far–reaching public attacks. These attacks can be complex and have the potential to deeply wound you and take you back to square one. Take the time to dig deep to not only build your resilience muscle but to also build your anti–fragile muscle. When life is good, we tend to drop out of therapy sessions and forget to do the self–care and spiritual and emotional resilience work but we never know what life may throw our way so a solid foundation is an important part of our armoury and toolkit for those unexpected times in life. If you have already unpacked your emotional baggage and managed any psychological trauma, pain or anger with a therapist and you are ready to move forward then consider building your emotional resilience by working with a life coach who can support you to identify how to cultivate and grow it and remain by your side, holding you gently accountable, as you do the work to achieve your goals for emotional resilience.

> *Resilience is not about toughening up, not about ignoring what we are feeling when we are hurt or experiencing pain, not about bottling it up and putting it in a Pandora's box. It's about acknowledging it, experiencing it and then doing the work of healing to prepare for our future success.*
>
> **#ColourFULL**

Intellectual resilience

Since I began to position myself as an expert and Thought Leader in the advancement of Women of Colour, I have seen others who saw the 'success' and have quickly rebranded to say they do the same thing but what they lack are the years of deep work in research and conversations to back their claim with integrity. What we often don't take into consideration is that by developing your knowledge and building intellectual resilience, you position your personal brand around trust. In professional relationships and business this is worth more than gold. I am not telling you to go out and get another degree or certification, what I am saying is to spend the time to firm up your knowledge and go deep on it – create your own unique understanding of the content. Intellectual resilience is not built by digesting content but by taking the time to pull it apart, form opinions, build on it, find the flaws, extend it and so on. Create intellectual knowledge and build resilience by positioning yourself as an expert in that space. Don't just be a consumer. Over time, you'll develop a reputation as a specialist rather than a generalist who regurgitates what's already out there. In a world overloaded with information, the people's careers that stand out are those that bring new thoughts and ideas to the table.

Work on your psychological, emotional, intellectual and spiritual fitness daily; be strategic and tactical. This internal step is imperative to building your solid foundation, your armoury and the tools you will use for what may in the future. When you do truly commit to moving the needle on your inner world you will build resilience and strength, and over time you will develop anti–fragility, the ability to get stronger and more powerful from leaning into hardship. The oppressor will have nothing on you, Sister! I have no doubt that you will become the leader that you always knew you were deep down; creating financial prosperity and success for yourself, your sisters, family, community and generations to come. When you are strong, we are strong. When you succeed, we succeed. You are never ever alone. You got this Sis, and I'm here believing in you and your incredible strength, loving you and cheering you on for the leader you are.

Share the quotes in this chapter with others
so that they too can be elevated, empowered and inspired.

Remember to tag Winitha so that we can reshare
your post with our global community.
Turn to p274 for Winitha's social media handles.

9

Colourism:
the battle within

"I am not tragically colored. There is no great sorrow dammed up in my soul, nor lurking behind my eyes...Even in the helter–skelter skirmish that is my life, I have seen that the world is to the strong regardless of a little pigmentation more or less. No, I do not weep at the world – I am too busy sharpening my oyster knife."

~ Zora Neale Hurston

There is a lot of content online and academia about race theory, colour bias, feminism, colonisation and colourism and I encourage you to research, read, learn, unlearn and relearn at your own pace. Here, I want to share some personal stories with you in the hope that it will give you comfort to then release any negative narratives you hold over yourself or your sisters in relation to skin colour. It is important to note that when I reference 'light' and 'dark' skin that these terms are understood in the context that skin tone is a gradient colour palette with no set definition for what is considered 'light' and what is 'dark.' Part of the problem with colourism is the terminology that stems from colonialism and therefore the systemic, societal and cultural beliefs that fuel it. For those that are unaware, colourism at its most simplistic form is discrimination or preferential treatment of people based on their skin colour. Alice Walker is often credited with first using the term and it was used in an essay in her book, *In Search of our Mothers' Gardens*. For Women of Colour there are added complexities when it comes to colourism such as identity and self-worth.

Throughout school, like most Women of Colour (regardless of tone or country), I was taunted for my skin colour. Doing this work in empowering Women of Colour has made me embrace my skin colour on a whole other level. I am proud of the colour in my skin. It's my identity and has been a part of my journey of self-acceptance and self-love. In my 20s, I was a professional dancer and did a lot of hip-hop dance. I would always joke and say that if you ever needed to find me in industry group photos, to look for the one 'brown dot' among 100 dancers and there I would be. Then I went to LA to train. I remember walking into a class and seeing the entire room filled with African Americans. I looked at their skin, then mine and felt a sudden delight came over my face. I had NEVER been in a public space where everyone also had more melanin. Of course, ethnically we had different origins and we were all from different cultures but the fact that I was in a room where there were also people with more melanin instead of less made me feel like I could...breathe. Like I could finally be myself. Even now, I am most myself and at home when in a room filled with Women and People of Colour.

Growing up, come summer, I would hear many disparaging comments from well-meaning aunties about the colour of my skin. In my immediate family, my brother and I are considered dark and I can easily get even browner when in the sun for only a few minutes. In summer I would go from a chocolate to a dark chocolate depending how much I sun-baked. According to them it was 'yuck' to be 'dark,' it was not seen as beautiful. In the grocery store I would see ointments manufactured by big multinational companies that were designed to lighten your skin; labelled with words like 'fair and lovely' and featuring Brown and Asian people with snow-white skin. I was confused as to why these products were in the ethnic stores and not in mainstream grocery stores since they were made and owned by White people. I now know why. For some sisters, the ideas around skin tone run so deep in our communities and cultures that we can be ostracised and bullied by our sisters, family and community for being too light or too dark. We run these false narratives in our mind and in turn promote them in our communities. For example, that the light-skinned sisters have it easy and get the jobs and gigs. We then shut doors on them and deliberately leave them out because of these bitter colourism beliefs. We believe that the dark-skinned sisters need to lighten their skin to be beautiful on their wedding day or that they got the job because they manipulated or fought their way up. We put our sisters down, sabotage their efforts and or leave them out of opportunities to advance in their career or be a part of the family and community because of our distorted colonised beliefs around skin colour and Eurocentric beauty ideals; beliefs that have never and will never serve us collectively; beliefs that diminish our power and propagate repression, suppression and oppression within our community. For some sisters they feel that they are too Black or Brown for White people and not Black or Brown enough for Black and Brown people. This dilemma exists especially for those who are mixed-raced and as a result they often experience added trauma around identity, belonging and social and cultural connection.

Colourism has infiltrated our world in many ways. According to the World Economic Forum, sales of skin-lightening products are projected to reach $8.9 billion by 2024 (World Economic Forum, *Colourism: How skin-tone bias affects racial equality at work*, 2020). White owned and operated beauty companies, the media and entertainment industries in our ethnic countries and in the Western diaspora have idealised White and lighter skin tones and created a form of psychological slavery with the ideals they manufacture and promote, further suppressing and oppressing us while capitalising on the very vulnerabilities they are responsible for causing. Skin-tone bias also exists in the workplace systemically and culturally and while some may argue that this is separate to racial bias, the fundamental context of this prejudice lies in the preference of those with lighter skin tones as opposed to darker skin tones particularly when it comes to meeting diversity and inclusion quotas. As Women of Colour, when we see this, it subconsciously, unconsciously and consciously affirms and promotes beliefs around colourism resulting in internalised suppression and or lateral violence. A vicious cycle created and maintained by the oppressor systemically and structurally.

Years ago, I dated a South Asian guy who had grown up in Australia and felt the pressure to be 'White.' Even though he was initially attracted to me for my absolute hotness, as we started dating, I noticed that he would talk to the lighter-skinned girls and put down the girls that had darker skin. When we went out, he would encourage me to wear a lighter colour foundation and stay out of the sun, telling me I was more beautiful when I my complexion was lighter. I allowed him to brainwash me with his bullshit and I found myself hiding from the sun, wearing a hat with paranoia of getting darker and using foundation that was way too light for my skin. Thank god I didn't stay with that douche bag. These ideals and beliefs have penetrated our cultures from generations gone to our current generation and are a direct result of colonisation and White supremacy. Colourism exists and it is keeping White supremacy in business. Colourism has not only infiltrated education, social and employment systems but also business and, sadly, our families and relationships, our communities and cultures. To revolt and create a revolution we must work together as a collective community to abolish colourism in our minds, our families, cultures and communities to reclaim our personal power and that for generations to come. We need to decolonise our own minds, yes even as Women of Colour.

> *I believe you were created just as you are for a reason and a purpose. Creation does not make mistakes.*
>
> *#ColourFULL*

Your skin colour was not a mistake; you are not too 'light' or too 'dark,' you are perfect. When you walk into a room and you are the only Woman of Colour, own that shit! Everyone looking at you or making stupid remarks about your identity? Great! Let them look, call it out to heal and reclaim your power. Leverage their attention to propel your career or business forward. Experience skin tone–bias at work? Work with a Woman of Colour career or executive coach to call it out, initiate grassroot campaigns like an activist and importantly, do the inner healing work. It's pivotal to your success and it's the life force of your leadership journey enabling you to reach your goals and become the leader you always knew you were on your terms unashamedly and unapologetically. Letting stories and narratives of past hurt and trauma based on your skin tone run around your head keeps you stuck and playing small, making you frustrated, anxious, resentful, angry and a whole lot of sad; negative emotions and beliefs that hold you back in a vicious cycle of trauma, hurt and pain. Left unhealed, these colourism experiences impact and change the capacity of your brain, it's called experience–dependent neuroplasticity.

Trying to hide your skin colour through lightening creams or foundation, sliding into the back corner at events, shrinking into your office cubicle or keeping your video off during virtual conferences is not the game that leaders play. Strut your stuff like Beyonce. There is nothing more powerful than a woman who is confident and owns who she is 100%. Confidence shifts the energy in the room, confidence encourages opportunities to float your way and it will keep you grounded as you step into leadership and do the deep work to transform the world. Confidence sends a strong message to those that persist in oppressing and suppressing you, your community and your sisters (through colourism and skin–tone bias) that you will no longer be defeated or allow those arrows to even come an inch near you or your sisters. Collectively we can wear them down and call–out their futile efforts of oppression by standing up. It's time for a revolution! You unlock your inner power when you accept every facet of who you are. When you unshackle and unleash your inner power you experience freedom, joy and fulfilment; putting you on track and creating traction to reach and achieve your leadership goals. The complete opposite of what the oppressor wants you to feel, think and do. Inner work and healing around colourism for ourselves, our cultures and communities is the kind of leadership that transforms the world but to transform, the world asks that we first transform ourselves. Reclaim your inner world; revolt and start a revolution.

Some of these beliefs run deep and for some of us there is a lot of healing, self–acceptance and self–love work that we need to do to reclaim our inner power but, ultimately, you get to choose what part you want your skin colour to play in your identity, your present and your future. You get to choose whether you will own it with pride or deny yourself of who you are and your uniqueness. WE GET TO CHOOSE. No one else does. Choose to take the time to heal from harmful colourism narratives towards yourself, those made towards you and those you direct at others. Work with a Woman of Colour psychologist or counsellor as part of this work and or engage in ancestral and cultural healing rituals. To heal from them is part of the process to decolonise our own minds; a coming back to who we truly are, created to be and always was. Take the steps that are needed to heal and reclaim you. I'm with you, Sister, every step of the way.

Share the quotes in this chapter with others
so that they too can be elevated, empowered and inspired.

Remember to tag Winitha so that we can reshare
your post with our global community.
Turn to p274 for Winitha's social media handles.

10

Self-care:
as activism and
preservation

*"Caring for myself is not self-indulgence, it is self-preservation,
and that is an act of political warfare."*

~ Audre Lorde

Self-care is doing the deep work because of self-love, neither of which can be created without taking time to nurture and nudge the areas of our lives that have been affected by individual, ancestral, collective, cultural and intergenerational trauma. Self-care without healing first is a band-aid solution; a resistance, procrastination and avoidance to do the real work of healing. Self-care without healing is an irresponsible use of our time and energy that we don't get back; it can only happen once we have done the deep work to heal our wounds and sought wisdom and diamonds from them; creating anti-fragility and resilience for our future leadership journey. We cannot thrive or fulfil our potential if we are wounded warriors. Healing is true self-care and the highest form of it. Without healing our journey will be one of continuous struggle, hardship and frustration. The wounds left open create space for self-sabotaging behaviour and resentment towards ourselves, leaving us lost in the vortex of our pain. Once lost, we need to work twice as hard to not only heal but also find ourselves. For some, the damage caused from denial and avoidance is eternal.

Real self-care is choosing practices where we feel safe, nurtured, loved, held, respected but also challenged. Find a space where you are challenged and seek support from someone who can convey truths and advice to you in a way that is deeply honest, compassionate, yet does not beat around the bush and is not watered down. This gloves-off approach is direct, raw and hits a punch. Sustainable healing, where wounds that have turned into scars stay so, can feel painful in its process. It's raw and when we feel the pain surface, my encouragement is to stay in that, not avoid or deny it but to stay in it long enough to do the transformational work you need to do to heal through the rituals and practices you pick up along the way. Breathe and self-soothe yourself through this process. Healing is not a one off, as Women of Colour we face many things in life and sometimes the bigger the success, the bigger the problems and challenges, the more healing work we find we need to do as a result of what these situations may bring or that it triggers old wounds realising that we have more healing to do in a particular situation. Healing is a practice, not a destination. It is something we do in good times to keep up our emotional, psychological and spiritual fitness and in bad times to stay on track and in motion. Give yourself grace, breathe through and surrender to the process as your inner self does the work of healing.

> \# *Through the process of giving attention to the parts of ourselves that are screaming for it silently, we honour ourselves with sovereignty.*
>
> **#ColourFULL**

When a baby cries, our heart tells us to go to it; we soothe, take the time to understand what is causing the distress and tend to the baby ASAP. Our lives are no less precious than that child. Your inner child is silently crying tears of sadness, bitterness, resentment, anger, frustration, disappointment, rage, confusion. Your inner child is distressed and is asking for your attention, love and tenderness. Sometimes this results in sickness and burnout; a signal that something is broken within us and demands our attention.

True self–care is deep: it's about releasing yourself, giving yourself permission to simply be you wholly as you are and to not seek from anyone or anything; hearing, seeing and valuing yourself first before seeking that from external sources. Living fully as you are, unapologetically, in all spaces with all people, unashamedly and 24/7. Making yourself your number one priority and truly being there for you. Talking to yourself soothingly and full of admiration and compassion. Implementing and maintaining healthy boundaries with everyone and everything including yourself. When you truly love yourself, you don't silence or dim your own light for anyone or anything including your own fears, negative emotions and false limiting beliefs. Regardless of fear, you choose not to suppress, repress, oppress or deny your being, allowing yourself to be free from self-sabotage, gaslighting yourself, destructive behaviour and red flag situations; you see the flag and you step away immediately.

Exercising, eating healthy, positive affirmations, journaling or sitting down to Netflix with wine and a side of your favourite ice-cream are supporters and enablers to self-care and keep us fit on the inside and out. However, they are not symptomatic of deep self-care. True deep self-care is taking actions to create a new paradigm and narrative regardless of your current reality. Choose to be defined and led by the vision of the future than the pain of the past. You must also look to and acknowledge the not-so-good parts of yourself, the parts of you that no longer serve yourself and or those around you that may be causing harm, with honesty and with self-care, love and compassion. Acknowledge and work on the parts of yourself with potential for growth to improve and live the best version of you every day, you deserve no less towards yourself. They say if you truly love someone, let them go. Deep self-love is being courageously able to let go of mindsets, beliefs, people, dreams, situations and things that do not enable us to live and breathe our best versions of ourselves because what is more important than fear, is the responsibility you have to yourself to live every moment to the fullest. Instead of allowing these things to weigh us down and hold us back, release them; you deserve the best life has to offer. In good times and bad, commit yourself to doing the deep intentional and focused work to bring your dreams and goals to life because you truly believe, to the depths of your core, that you deserve it.

True self-care is sticking at the process and taking the time to work through the unsexy stuff; the stuff that you don't feel like doing or enjoy doing but that is required to achieve your goal. Improve and optimise the internal mindsets and beliefs and the external systems you will use to achieve your goals and dreams because it's the process that's the journey and the very means that will determine if you will reach your destination or not. And by optimising it you are valuing your time and energy by ensuring the foundation, the process, is the most efficient and effective it can be. That is how you will improve yourself. Small bad habits lead to long–term regret so conquer them while they are small and receive abundance and peace long–term. Self–care is sticking to the process during the hard times and putting in the work required to navigate and overcome them. You know it's the hard times that help shape and sharpen your skills and mindset to prepare you to play a bigger game in the future with bigger rewards.

Overcoming obstacles and challenges is another avenue to self–love and self–care because it brings awareness for what we refuse to endure and builds our inner courage in those moments, opportunities for us to choose no longer put up but to stand up, unashamedly and unapologetically. Choose growth.

The Universe and God only give you what you feel you are worthy to receive.

#ColourFULL

In order for you to feel worthy of receiving, well that's a you–job, not a God–job. Meet the universe halfway. Let go of expectations of outcomes for how it is exactly meant to be because life is a marathon, not a sprint. Expectations poison your motivation, self–worth and personal power so focus on the process and what you can control, take the next step and then the next.

Real leaders do not deny their experiences and they have the courage to step boldly into those inner spaces that we often avoided in fear; spaces that they may be fearful of but know are needing of attention in order to reach their goals. Warrior leadership is knowing that in order to become a leader that impacts and influences, you must first lead, impact and influence your inner self, your soul. The warrior leaders who have done the deep healing work persecute and wield the greatest power. Internal power. You feel it when they walk into a room; when you spend five minutes in their presence; when you hear them speak. They shift an entire room and command their attention. Through the process of deep healing, they have become a channel for a source and power greater than them (self–transcendence). This is the work that a mere few venture out on and most give up on; persisting in the journey of healing because of the knowledge that this is real, true and deep self–care, a gift of self–love and the only way to be a leader. Safety of others is a priority so they lead from their scars, not from their open wounds. Through the process of healing, they've self–actualised, transformed and transcended. The journey of healing has enabled them to truly understand their absolute power and harness it so they lead with courage, unashamedly, unapologetically.

Start your journey to self–love. Invest your time and energy in your ideas and go for it. Roll up your sleeves and do the work even if it feels like a hot mess at times. Refuse for a dream to simply stay a dream and do the work to turn it into a reality. Be yourself, unashamedly and unapologetically, good bad, ugly bits and all. Be real and have honest and courageous conversations with yourself. Don't choose to let your thoughts hold you captive. Free yourself, let yourself go after that idea; after that dream; after that goal; after you. Let go, let in, accept, surrender. Lean in and fully commit to your healing, to DEEP self–care, no excuses, shame, playing the blame game and no justifications. Then only, you will truly love you. Then only, you will lead powerfully, fully yourself from dusk–to–dawn transforming the world one day, one step and one action at a time.

Self–love and self–care are not a feeling, they are an ACTION. Love is not all honeymoons and stardust. Love is sometimes hard and challenging; requiring constant realignment, resetting, healing, nudging and nurturing. So too is self–care. Show yourself some self–care by releasing who you are and destined to be by taking action today. It's not being indulgent, it's taking care of you, liberating you, owning you, freeing you, loving you. Self–care is activism so revolt, Sister and start a revolution.

*Share the quotes in this chapter with others
so that they too can be elevated, empowered and inspired.*

*Remember to tag Winitha so that we can reshare
your post with our global community.
Turn to p274 for Winitha's social media handles.*

11

Get clear, get focused: start with you

"You can't be hesitant about who you are."

~ Viola Davis

I want to challenge your ideals around success right now. Ask yourself why you want to be successful: what will it really give you? Be honest and courageous with yourself to dive deep beyond the surface response and into your inner truth. Why do you really want it, what is it really about, what will it give you and how will it make you feel in attaining it? In those answers you will understand what it is that your soul is craving, crying out for.

A coach I was once working with asked me, 'Why do you want to be successful?' As a leadership and business coach myself and someone who is hyper-aware and psycho-analytical, I knew I was cornered with this question; there was nowhere to go or hide. I was afraid to answer because doing so meant admitting the truth to myself. I took a deep courageous breath and leaned into the process for my greater good growth and learning. 'To show myself that I am good enough that I can do it, that I deserve it and that I am smart.' Immediately after I asked myself, 'Is it worth it? And can negative emotions and experiences be leveraged to attain goals?' My answer is yes, in terms of getting you kick started into motion and to develop a rhythm to your action and journey, but to use that as fuel in the long-term is toxic and can be harmful to your sense of self, identity and potentially to others who you are responsible for leading. A more fulfilling, freeing, healthy, healing and powerful place to start is: how do you want to feel and how could you create that feeling in your life? I knew within myself, in the anecdote above, that going after my goals to prove to myself and others that I was smart wasn't a healthy approach to attaining career and business success and is certainly not great self-leadership or a responsible way to then lead others. After that coaching session, I pondered and felt that inner truth surface-up. True success and the pursuit of goals is really about the feeling that we assume lies underneath the goal, for example we may want to feel joy, peace, freedom, fulfilment and belonging. So, it makes sense to set goals from a place of feeling as opposed to the attainment of things or to prove something to ourselves and others. To create a career and life that you want is about the feeling, it's actually got nothing to do with the outcome!

# #

'We are chasing the feeling behind the goal, not the goal itself'
Danielle LaPorte

#ColourFULL

It's merely a physical manifestation of what we think will give us that desired feeling. In our quest to be a leader, we are chasing our assumption of how we think being a leader will make us feel, as opposed to leadership for leaderships sake.

I recommend this approach to my students in the LevelUP program as well. Our first session is always around setting clear intentional, focused and positive goals that have a sense of aspiration and purpose to them and leave people inspired and energised. Students will often come in with their lists of goals but I always ask them to 'Wipe the table of their life clear' for the first session; we leave any pre–existing expectations, experiences, goals, dreams, ideas or previous notions, assumptions and definitions of success at the door. We get down to the nitty gritty and unpack it deeply. I challenge them, hold them accountable while holding the space to enable them to get really deep to allow space for their inner truth to come out. How do they want to feel? Truly feel? Try it now; what would come up if you were to get quiet, get still, take a few deep breaths with your eyes gently closed and ask yourself, 'How do I want to feel?' From there we can brainstorm all the things we could possibly do to feel that way. No box is left unturned and we give permission for the big, the small the normal and the weird and wacky. We then look for the themes and at this stage of the process I start co–collaborating with the student to put words together from this work intuitively and psycho-analytically to form a goal statement. As I lead this process and we create their goal statement I watch as a massive smile comes across their face as they read it out loud and this is when I know we've nailed it. It's like they've found that thing they've been searching for their entire life, they can breathe. We've reached The Holy Grail. They've come home.

Starting from a place of feeling first ensures that when you reach your goal, you aren't disappointed by the fact that the goal didn't give you (make you feel) what you assumed it would, or worse, you realise that it's actually not what you want. Because we only have an idea, right? We THINK that by doing X that we will truly feel, for example, happy and fulfilled but it's an assumption, not a fact. What we are actually chasing is happiness and fulfilment and technically that can be achieved through a range of things, not just the current career path, business concept, idea or goal in your head. It isn't until we are doing the thing that we think will give us our desired feelings that we know for sure and until then it's simply an assumption, a hypothesis. Your view of the world is informed and limited by your past and current experiences. To get clear on how you want to feel tap into your intuition, your superpower, and let it guide you in the direction of your life by immersing yourself in a range of varied experiences. Talk to people who are doing what you aspire to do; ask to shadow them a few days a week or take on a short-term role, contract job or internship, paid or volunteer; attend industry and networking events and conferences.

In order to understand how it makes you feel, consider how you can dip your toes by:

Reading and researching.

Watching a video/documentary.

Listening to a podcast.

Creating an experience.

\#   Talking to a leader in a role you aspire to do.

\#   Completing a certain action or activity in that space.

\#   Immersing yourself in an environment such as an industry event.

\#   Interacting with people, places, things for example through a secondment.

\#   Running an experiment to test the idea on a small scale.

\#   Joining a community.

Listen to your intuition and if you are confused, speak to a coach, mentor, trusted adviser, friend or psychologist to guide and support you. I believe that, as Women of Colour, our biggest superpower is our intuition. Intuition is fed through individual, collective, ancestral and cultural experiences that are carried in our spirit, DNA and community. By immersing ourselves in an experience, we provide our intuition with the data necessary to make an informed decision about what is truly going to work for us in the present and future and what's not. We can check if X will make us feel Y; as imperfect humans in an imperfect world we only know so much. The first time I went to university, I decided to focus my business degree on supply chain management. About a year and a half into the course, I thought it would be best to work in the industry before I graduated so that if I didn't like it, I could at least switch to another major and not waste another 18 months of my life. And so that is exactly what I did and have continued to do in other areas of my life. When contemplating career changes, I have done short internships, work experience and shadowed people to get a sense of whether it was what I really wanted to do. It has been an invaluable practice.

I used to think it would be absolute bliss to work for a certain organisation as the CEO. I used to drive by the offices wishing and then one day it came true. I ended up hating that organisation and the board. The experience made me realise that what I truly wanted to do was not be the CEO of an organisation but to be the CEO of my life. By immersing myself in that experience, I was able to discern that that career path was not for me. We often think that the way to advance is by going 'up' but it doesn't have to be – you can go down, sideways, diagonally, even in circles. Leadership comes in all forms and isn't restricted by job titles. You need to find your own jam, your own definition of success and leadership that will give you all those juicy feelings you desire and crave, and the only way to find that is by immersing yourself in experiences. Give yourself permission to pursue that which makes you feel all the feelings you want to feel. This is true success and leadership for us.

Freedom for Women of Colour is not necessarily about being the CEO of a large multinational or a manager of one thousand employees. It's about the freedom to feel what we choose to feel unashamedly and unapologetically, fearlessly and courageously; to create and pursue a life of design and not of default. To intentionally and strategically create our lives and careers, driving our own experiences and making life happen for us, not to us. It makes sense, in this short life that we have, to create goals from a place of feeling first. This is the path to clarity and focus and is the process we return to whenever we may be feeling confused, overwhelmed, frustrated, stressed, triggered, sad, angry, discontent, resentful in pain and unfocused. All we need to ask ourselves is, 'Is this making me feel how I want to feel?' and if not, what will? Do something about it to make it work for you, to make you feel how you want to feel. By meeting those desires, it creates the foundation for meaningful, deep, sustainable and true success in a way that nourishes and grows us, unleashing our inner power as we step into the fullest version of ourselves. The toughest gig in our leadership journey is not leading others. It's leading ourselves to fulfil the desired direction of our own lives and potential. This is true leadership, self–leadership, leading from the inside out. It is only when we are living and breathing as the fullest version of ourselves that we are then able to lead masterfully with grace and integrity, and execute like a pro. It is only when we feel how we want to feel that we free ourselves from the modern–day shackles of psychological slavery and the burdens of those that came before us and thereby free future generations. This is true real leadership. The kind of leadership that leaves a legacy and transforms the world.

Get clear and get a sharp focus on what leadership really means to you: unpack how you assume leadership and success will make you feel and how you really want to feel and set goals from that place first. Once you get clear and focused, this is what is going to make you the kind of leader that shifts the energy in the room as they enter it. The kind of leader that influences strategically with heart and mind. The kind of leader that creates true, deep, long–term, sustainable and meaningful impact in the world. This is the stuff that real leadership is made of and this is the leadership of the future. So, get clear and get focused on how you really want to feel in your life. You only have one life, make your time here count.

Share the quotes in this chapter with others
so that they too can be elevated, empowered and inspired.

Remember to tag Winitha so that we can reshare
your post with our global community.
Turn to p274 for Winitha's social media handles.

12

Reclaim your name: and power up

"You tell me to quiet down 'cause my opinions make me less beautiful, but I was not made with a fire in my belly so I could be put out. I was not made with a lightness on my tongue so I could be easy to swallow. I was made heavy half blade and half silk—difficult to forget and not easy for the mind to follow."

~ Rupi Kaur

Oftentimes people ask me, 'Do I need to change my name to get ahead or get a job?' and my advice is no. Absolutely not. Baby, make them say your name. Reclaim all that belongs to you including your name. I know it's hard, but collectively we can't keep giving into the system. When we do we become part of the problem and we perpetuate it. Since I was born everyone called me by my middle name, Michelle. My mum called me Michelle because she was scared kids would tease me if I used my first name, Winitha, as it was 'ethnic sounding.' Turns out Winitha is actually Dutch.

In Sri Lanka, aspects of colonisation from the Dutch, Portuguese, English and French (and god knows whatever countries that also invaded) have seeped into our ancestral culture. Names were one of them; my last name, Bonney, is another result of colonisation. When I started doing this work, I decided to start using my first name, Winitha. The name my mother gave me, after my dad, Winfred. Some people take liberties and call me 'Winnie' and I let them only rarely because it reminds me of Nelson Mandela's wife. But the 99.99%? I ask them to call me Winitha and to pronounce it correctly. I'm sure that many people also take liberties with your name; shortening it or giving you an entirely new name that is easier for them to pronounce. Perhaps they have mistaken you for the other Woman of Colour in the office and called you their name, or when people ask your name you tell them, 'Just call me [something that sounds more Anglo–Saxon or a shortened version that is not my name].' We do this so as not to burden others but do we ask White people to shorten their names or to give us an easier name to pronounce? I mean that's equity, right? If we are expected to shorten or change our names to make it easier to pronounce for White people, shouldn't they do the same thing for us? Clearly, they are not. Standing for and drawing the boundary lines for equity requires you to do it in the small things, setting the tone and expectation for the bigger things. Now, there are some reasons why you might change your name. If you don't like your name and want to change it, change it. But don't change your name for someone else. Ask them to say your name. Enough has been taken away from us as Women of Colour. Your name was given to you for a reason. It's a blessing not a curse.

Do not reduce your worth or devalue yourself to make White people feel more comfortable or to make their life easier – I mean do you see them actively doing that for you on a daily basis? Refuse to carry the burden of the emotional tax we as Women of Colour pay on a daily basis. Don't change your name in the hope of getting a job or an opportunity, let alone to make a non–Woman of Colour comfortable because they are struggling to pronounce your name correctly. This is a simple example of the many ways we choose to continue to enslave ourselves to mindsets, beliefs and thoughts that do not serve us by compromising on our identity and our essence; internalised suppression. When you make a stand and ask for equity in the small and big things and put in healthy boundaries that preserve and grow your self–worth and value, you free yourself. The problem with changing your name or allowing others to change it is this: know, that every time you let people know that they can call you by your nickname or allow people to call you a shortened form of your name without your consent, you are perpetuating racism and systemic discrimination. Again, if you let them do it in the small things then you give permission for them to do it in the bigger things. I also put my hand up as guilty.

When was the last time a White person told you their name was John and you called them Jo instead because it was easier for you to pronounce?

#ColourFULL

When was the last time they changed their name on their resume or LinkedIn profile just to get a job or connect with you? If we don't ask that of White people and they don't do that for us then why on Earth do we allow them to do it to us, or change our name to make them feel comfortable or get a foot in the door? A life of respect and integrity to oneself is a life well lived versus the glamour of a certain job, cash in the bank or leadership title.

Every time we give people permission to shorten our name and or call us by a nickname, what we are essentially saying is, 'Yes, it's ok to deny me my simple right of calling me by my birth name, go ahead and deny me of everything else!' and so they change the name and, in the process, disempower the next sister and the next. We let them open the gate to racism and discrimination by a teeny–tiny bit, enabling them to then push it wide open instead of keeping the gate firmly shut by putting our boundaries down for the sake of our self–preservation, self–worth, self–value, healing, personal power and ultimately, self–love. Every time we choose to change our name and call ourselves Michelle instead of Winitha, or to give ourselves a western–sounding first or last name, we are feeding into the system. We are telling them it's ok to strip us of our identity. Stand by your name. Let them get it wrong, and correct them every time. It may feel exhausting but racism is like a toxic fungus that spreads rapidly. It only takes one spoiled apple to spoil the whole basket. Learning someone's name is simply respect. I also struggle to say some names. Once, while driving with a friend for three hours to visit a Zimbabwean sister, I practiced her name the entire way there to roll it with my tongue the way my friend could to get it nuanced and just right. Rolling my tongue doesn't come naturally to me but I practiced.

Use your name. Stick to your name. Flaunt it, own it, be it and make it your personal brand. Put those boundaries down and let me repeat…self–preservation! Make them say your name. Enough has been taken from you. Do not be silent; speak up and out, reclaim your name and it will give you the courage, confidence and conviction to reclaim everything else that belongs to you resulting in personal power and healing. When you do, you send a strong message to those you work with and to the oppressor that you will no longer endure oppression in the small things, let alone the big things. Proudly wear the name given to you and reclaim it.

Share the quotes in this chapter with others
so that they too can be elevated, empowered and inspired.

Remember to tag Winitha so that we can reshare
your post with our global community.
Turn to p274 for Winitha's social media handles.

PART 2

REWRITE YOUR OUTER WORLD

13

I speak English: recruiters and English as an additional language

"You wanna fly…you got to give up the shit that weighs you down."

~ Toni Morrison

'In the application, I'm not asked for my name but where I went to school or previously worked or studied at university is a dead giveaway that I am from overseas. Do I need to call the recruiter to let them know I speak English fluently?' 'I have an accent and I feel that people can't always understand what I say, I'm taking classes to get better but is my accent stopping me from getting a job?'

These are some of the questions I get asked frequently. What I sense is the real essence of the question is: how can language concerns be addressed directly with recruiters? Have you called a recruiter before or after an electronic application so that they can hear your voice and know that you can speak English to reclaim your personal power from their bias? Have you called them to strongly pitch your skills and expertise? This is one way you could navigate the White structures and systems that seek to oppress us. Calling before you apply for a job puts your name in their mind and possibly your resume at the top of the electronic pile. It potentially directly addresses any biases they may have, reclaims your personal power, flips the power dynamic, shifts the focus on the value you bring and shows that you are proactive. However, from this seemingly powerless position, to self–preserve and heal as a matter of priority, my suggestion to you is to first take a moment to self–soothe your concern that it was your accent or the fact that English is an additional language that prevented you or might prevent you from getting the job. If you do call, move the conversation to quickly re–focus the recruiter on your skills and experience with 80% of the conversation spent doing a hard sell of yourself. If you are feeling bold then tell them directly, 'I've had difficulty getting a job and I feel it's because most recruiters, after looking at my application, make the assumption that I can't speak English or that my accent will be an issue. As a proud Woman of Colour, this is one of the barriers that we face in the journey towards equity and equality. We know that people that speak more than one language are more skilled in other areas; the fact that I speak more than one language demonstrates my ability to pick up complex information quickly and execute masterfully. If you have a few minutes, I'd like to quickly take you through my experience and qualifications and get your feedback as to whether I would be suitable for the role. How does this sound?'

If you don't get the job, call the recruiter and ask for honest and direct feedback as to why you didn't get it. Even better, take action and call right after applying to ask for five minutes of their time to discuss your suitability for the job, steering the conversation towards your pitch (the value you will add through your expertise). In this conversation also ask for next steps and timelines in the recruitment process as well as information on what they are doing to ensure the process (from recruitment to induction to company culture) is inclusive and without bias. In this empowered action, by calling or meeting with them directly and calling out any bias or discrimination gracefully you are putting your foot forward while inviting them to see your brilliance. By calling out their behaviour directly, you are letting them know that you are fully aware that the reason you didn't get that opportunity is due to discriminatory biases viewed on their end as assumptions. You have nothing to prove, however, when you connect with them directly and call it out you take up the opportunity to reclaim your power for you, your community and your sisters. You also create the opportunity to amplify your power and rewrite your job and promotion application processes by tweaking your strategy and actions in response to feedback in terms of what is considered 'of value' to them and whether that aligns to you or not. But hey, if you don't feel like you have the emotional bandwidth to do that or that you don't need to prove anything to anyone, especially to a White person, that you can speak English then that's ok too. I understand finding a job can be hard. I know systemic discrimination and racism exists and that people have biases when they see our faces, name or the countries where we previously worked and studied. However, know this, if an employer does not give you a job or promotion because of your accent or because English is an additional language then they are not the right employer for you; save yourself from a disastrous situation. Don't award and perpetuate a system that seeks to shut us out and treat us as less than with your priceless gifts, talents, energy and expertise.

Life is short. Don't give your pearls to pigs.

#ColourFULL

Call them directly either before you apply for a job or after and gracefully and respectfully call out the elephant in the room. It may not change anything but in that moment, you have ensured that your voice is heard – and that is the only voice that matters. Every time we don't stand up, we lose a little bit of our power, self–worth and value. Reclaim what rightfully belongs to you, your personal power and identity; what makes you, you. Stand up, call it out, speak to it directly and keep putting yourself forward. Rewrite and revolutionise your game plan for applying for jobs and promotions. Think outside the box and utilise your brilliance, your superpowers – all that magic that makes you an incredible Woman of Colour.

Share the quotes in this chapter with others
so that they too can be elevated, empowered and inspired.

Remember to tag Winitha so that we can reshare
your post with our global community.
Turn to p274 for Winitha's social media handles.

14

Racism:
was what they said racist?

"Justice is about making sure that being polite is not the same thing as being quiet. In fact, often times, the most righteous thing you can do is shake the table."

~ Alexandria Ocasio-Cortez

Trust your inner intuition. As women, we can often feel the pressure to not get emotional, create 'drama,' 'overreact' or 'cause a fuss.' As Women of Colour, we might feel the pressure to not bring out the 'race card' or behave in a way that reinforces the cultural and gender stereotype. Whatever it is, tell those thoughts to get back on the bus and keep moving; they got off at the wrong stop. My invitation to you is to no longer accept others' views as your own. Form your own mind. Listen to your inner intuition, wisdom, God. These unhelpful thoughts can often lead us to question ourselves and rationalise words, situations and people away, essentially gaslight ourselves. We may even engage in tone policing oneself and being overly harsh and self–critical towards ourselves, thinking how we should not have said or done whatever to provoke that situation. We create excuses and justifications for their terrible and idiotic behaviour and play the blame and shame game with ourselves. We may remain silent, adding to the problem and deepening our own internalised suppression. I often wonder if this is because we do not want to accept the reality that we have been discriminated against and what that means for us so we shut Pandora's box from a place of fear of triggering past trauma, negative emotions and limiting beliefs. We can become so conditioned by the system around us that those comments and remarks are often heard as normal, acceptable and not with any racist intent at all. We become immune to them. As Kemi Nekvapil said to me once, 'What was previously acceptable is no longer accepted.'

I get it, it's never nice to think that Karen, who we thought was an ally, is actually a racist. Regardless if it was conscious, unconscious, subconscious or whatever the hell people will use to excuse themselves, it's usually point–blank racism and Sis, do you know it. If you have to ask me or another sister whether it was, the answer is probably yes. You might say, 'It didn't sound right,' 'It didn't sit well with me' or that it bothered you.

If you are questioning yourself as to whether what happened was discriminatory then, in my experience, it was.

#ColourFULL

Don't gaslight yourself. You will only deepen your wounds and subconsciously give others permission to also gaslight you too, while being exactly where the oppressor wanted you to be; suffering in internalised suppression resulting in a withdrawal of personal power, potential, dreams and goals. As they say, how you treat yourself gives permission for others to treat you the same way. And the fact you are second guessing yourself is in itself a form of subtle and covert inequity that exists between non–Women of Colour and us. This is why speaking to another Women of Colour coach, mentor and friend is so important; they can hear when you are gaslighting yourself, hold the space to your healing and help you craft and execute a strategy that will amplify your voice and career in a revolt of what you just experienced; your revolution. Leverage the experience that is happening within you and your inner wisdom by uncovering the wisdom and diamonds from your wounds and using the situation as a training ground; an opportunity to build anti–fragility and resilience to prepare you for your leadership journey.

For me, when it happens fast and I walk away dizzy, wondering what the hell just happened...only to kick myself after, I give myself some grace, acknowledge that I am also learning, and then work with another Woman of Colour on the steps I can take to self–preserve, to heal and then to reclaim my voice and power. For example, do I take the person aside and have a conversation; put in a formal complaint to HR; send their manager an email; let it go for the sake of self–preservation and healing? I get clear on strategy and execute masterfully. This is my armour. In my early days, I strategised with an executive coach to create a script which I practiced with them, and then approached the person. I would walk into the conversation imagining that I was in a protective bubble and, if they choose to react negatively, I imagined a mirror between them and me, facing them and their words and behaviours bouncing right back at them. Other times I'd promptly timestamp the conversation and send it as a formal complaint to HR, CC'ing their manager. The script would include something along the lines of: 'I want to let you know that what X said [insert their comment] was racist and symptomatic of the culture that exists in this company. I believe that you as an organisation can and will do better towards People of Colour. Psychological and cultural safety is a priority and, if needed, I will be required to take further action. If you are not of the opinion that what they said is racist, then unfortunately this isn't something I am able to have a conversation with you about or educate you on. I can, however, refer you to a Woman of Colour and Thought Leader in this space that can (Winitha Bonney: www.winitha.com). I don't expect you to understand it all right now, but I do expect you to hear and respect what I've just said and communicate your plan of how you will ensure that as a company we are creating safe, equitable spaces for Women and People of Colour. There is a heap of resources online if you need support and Winitha can point you in the right direction. Thanks, and I look forward to hearing from you soon.'

Other times, depending on the context, I choose not to give my pearls to pigs because it's either not worth it or, knowing them, I'd be adding fuel into a fire that would end up burning me. Your only responsibility in these situations is your emotions and how you choose to respond internally and externally that will either bring healing and personal power to you or additional trauma. That's it. Always document incidents with the date, time, people who were there and the conversation as verbatim as you can recall it. Stay strategic and two steps ahead in case you decide to make a formal complaint and they then try to performance manage you out of your job. Back yourself and cover your gorgeous backside.

Listen to your inner intuition. Trust yourself and speak out to reclaim your personal power, to rewrite your outer world and your leadership journey. This is your revolution. These experiences are a training ground for when we do step into leadership where we may have added responsibilities as well as a highly visible public profile meaning you will have to endure more complex and consistent office politics and games, discrimination, racism, challenges, problems and pressures. Sharpen your armour and your weaponry. Learn to tune into your intuition, to identify and hear it clearly and to respect and honour your inner and outer voice. Learn to create resilience against 'reacting' and to instead proactively strategise and masterfully execute when you experience racist and discriminative incidents in and outside the workplace. Welcome these hardships and challenges as opportunities and a time to create and build anti–fragility, practice your skills, refine your strategy and craft your revolution to prepare you for your brilliant leadership future ahead. And above all else, if you think it was racist, then it was.

Share the quotes in this chapter with others
so that they too can be elevated, empowered and inspired.

Remember to tag Winitha so that we can reshare
your post with our global community.
Turn to p274 for Winitha's social media handles.

📘 🐦 in 📷 👻 📌

15

Inclusive organisations: are they really?

"Excellence is the best deterrent to racism or sexism."

~ Oprah Winfrey

Many of us want to know which organisations are inclusive and safe for us to work in. In my thought leadership practice, I get involved with leaders of large and small organisations to help them improve their inclusive work practices and create equity and equality for People of Colour. Through this work, I know that no organisation is 100% inclusive because we are imperfect people living in an imperfect world. Some Women of Colour have a swell time in a department while others in a neighbouring department have a hellish time! Organisations are made up of people and your experience will vary depending on the people you work and interact with on a daily basis as well as the culture of the organisation and the systems and policies that govern it. Any organisation can have the best intention but ultimately it is up to the people it employs to choose to be inclusive and equitable. Things don't change unless people choose to change. The system won't change unless people decide that it must and get to work dismantling and decolonising it.

Right now, the flavour in diversity and inclusion work is around the gender equality pay gap. The work that is happening is the White female, straight, cis, able boded equity kind of work; White feminism. There are no organisations that I know of that can proudly say they have achieved significant gains in creating equity and equality for Women and People of Colour, Black, Brown and First Nations people. The organisational and structural journey to true inclusion and equity is long, arduous and complex and can't be achieved with a simple strategy in one year let alone a few days of training; it takes years and years and mountains of money, time and energy. J.P. Morgan and Ben and Jerry's are organisations that make me think, 'Ok, I see you...' but I'm positive even they have more dismantling work to do and still get it wrong sometimes. I'm not saying that we need to be negative and think the whole world is doom and gloom or out to get us but I do think the labelling of workplaces as entirely 'inclusive organisations' is entertaining an impossible idea, well, for our generation at least. Just because an organisation champions accessibility or gender equality, does not mean that they are inclusive in all areas of diversity and in all areas of the business let alone in the sense of what true inclusion is and looks like. What this actually means is that they are champions of accessibility and most likely White Feminism; full stop. Likewise, posting a statement that 'Black Lives Matter' doesn't mean they have done anything internally. It actually doesn't really mean anything at all and that's why we call this performative allyship. In my experience, the companies that are choosing to do the hard, difficult, challenging and uncomfortable work of dismantling discrimination and decolonising systems of oppression don't shout it from the mountain tops. Instead, they've got their bums up and heads down, deep in the work of looking after their people and the community around them; it's not as clear or easy to see as feel–good fist pumping social media campaigns.

I want to give you a few ideas for how you can take empowered action to find which organisations might have an equitable culture that will value you as a Woman of Colour.

Talk to the Women of Colour who work in the company

What never lies, are the Women and People of Colour who actually work in these organisations and companies day in, day out. Use your existing networks or find Women of Colour on LinkedIn to ask for a private and confidential conversation about what it's like to work in that organisation or department as a Woman of Colour. Ask them for other information about the company: is it advanced in reducing bias in their recruiting processes and systems or are they old fashioned? What is the level of bias in the organisation and are they inclusive in other areas of diversity? What's their current approach to equity, inclusion and diversity? What is the culture like? Is it psychologically and culturally safe? Do they provide career and leadership progression opportunities for Women of Colour? Are there any in middle or senior management?

Do your research and trawl the company's online content

You can learn volumes about companies and organisations online. Look to see if the company and the people it employs post online content that demonstrates the values and principles of great inclusion practice and aligns to your own values. Find their LinkedIn company page and track their posts and find the people that work there and track their posts to see what content they have engaged in to figure out what the culture may be like. Look to see what you can physically identify, as the percentage of Women of Colour that work in that organisation. You can generally tell from Christmas function photos, through their website, annual report or by looking at the profiles of people who have tagged their LinkedIn account to work in that company. Have a look at how many years they have been there and what level they are at. Have a look at the organisation's ratings on Glassdoor and read the comments. Look at their executive team and board, is there representation from People of Colour? What is their view on equity, diversity and inclusion looking at their annual report? Is a strategic priority and imperative or an afterthought? Or not even thought of at all? Use your judgement. Use your intuition.

Look at the organisation's people reports, media and other online content. Is there a spotlight on their inclusion work; do they have a budget line for it and is it substantial; what is their strategic focus; is equity, diversity and inclusion its own standalone business function and where and who does it report to? Do they mention equity?

When they do talk about diversity and inclusion, be your savvy, brilliant clever self and tap into your lived experience to read between the lines of what they are really saying.

#ColourFULL

Is it one sided; is it White–female equality heavy, does it break gender equality down with an intersectional lens or does it lump everyone into one homogeneous group?

Call the recruiter or manager and be bold with your questions

I know that many White people feel very uncomfortable talking about racism. The mere word, let alone the terms Woman or Person of Colour has them twitching from nervousness like they're sitting on a cushion of pins. I acknowledge in that moment that they may be learning how to navigate these conversations like a new language, and that in learning a new language they may get stuff wrong, make mistakes or communicate absolute nonsense that's quite offensive. If I have the emotional bandwidth and their heart and intention is in the right place, I generally let White people know at the very start of the conversation that 'This is a safe, kind, respectful and nurturing space for you to get it wrong. I need you to make mistakes, be clunky and uncomfortable and struggle through it if you have to. That's the only way we can unlearn to learn and relearn. I'm going to hold this space with lots of love and kindness for you as we go on this journey, does that sound ok?' You can edit this and use something of that effect when calling the recruiter or manager. And then there are idiots and I don't bother with them at all. You know who they are.

If you are feeling sleuthy, contact the Diversity & Inclusion person at the organisation or find them on LinkedIn. Warm them up first by having a candid conversation with them and then go in for the ask. Ask them what they are doing for Women of Colour, if they understand the term and its history and whether there many Women of Colour working in that organisation and if so at what level. Ask them from the context of, 'I've been thinking about X and I'd like to share ideas on inclusion. Do you have 10 minutes this Friday?' Then aim to meet them face to face or over Zoom. 70% of communication is non–verbal so lead with that statement and question, if you have the capacity to ease them into. Alternatively, you can generally see how comfortable they are with uncomfortable conversations by cutting out the fat and getting straight to the conversation. HR recruiters from organisations with safe inclusive cultures don't react to that question with shock, resentment or nervousness. Those who haven't unpacked their privilege or are from the organisations that haven't even looked at racism are generally pretty obvious to pick from their reaction to your question.

If you feel nervous about asking directly, my encouragement is to be candid, 'I know this may be an uncomfortable question for some as it is uncomfortable for me to ask but rather than asking the obvious questions, I want to ask something that is deeply important to me and reflective of my values. This speaks to my resilience and integrity as an employee and my ability to have difficult conversations with grace and respect in the pursuit of growth and progress. I'd like to ask X.' Let them know that, as a Woman of Colour, you need to ensure that the organisational is psychologically and culturally safe and enquire as to what they are currently doing to ensure this, 'I'm really passionate about inclusion as a Woman of Colour and am interested to know what you are currently doing to create equity and equality in the workplace for people from diverse backgrounds. Do you have any examples you could share with me? What practices do you utilise to ensure your culture is safe for all employees? How are you creating an inclusive business?'

Unfortunately, there is no predetermined way to measure or assess if an organisation is inclusive of Women of Colour. My suggestion is to trust your inner wisdom and your intuition; it's never wrong and the more you use it the stronger it becomes. The brain and intuition are like a muscle, flex it. Trust that the Universe, God or whatever you believe in has your back and will protect and guide you to a job and organisation in which you can truly thrive and that will progress you along your leadership journey. That your organisation will be a fun, inclusive and safe space for an exceptional Woman of Colour like you to become the powerful, impactful and influential leader you know you are.

Share the quotes in this chapter with others
so that they too can be elevated, empowered and inspired.

Remember to tag Winitha so that we can reshare
your post with our global community.
Turn to p274 for Winitha's social media handles.

f 𝕏 in ⃝ 👻 ⓟ

16

Gaslighting: protect and reflect to deflect

"You've got to learn to leave the table when love's no longer being served. I'm a real rebel with a cause."

~ Nina Simone

There are many strategies and tactics that the system uses to keep us stagnant, stuck and suffering from the effects of, what I call, modern–day psychological slavery as well as ancestral and intergenerational trauma. In order to know how to beat it we must understand how it works, operates and what it thrives off, as well as its impact on us and how it shows up daily. We must be aware and understand its intricacies. From the most subtle attacks and tactics to the most overt; from the individual level to structural and systemic. The most rampant yet subtle tactic used by the oppressor is gaslighting. I'm no psychologist but I have had my fair share of gaslighters in my life. There was a moment when, after years of constant gaslighting in all areas of my life, it all got a bit too much and I physically hit my head against a wall, wondering if I could jolt it back to normality. I had started questioning my sanity and was rapidly disintegrating mentally. I did see a psychologist, hoping she would fix me, and when she labelled one of the main perpetrators as a bully – that shook me firmly back into reality. I was not the problem; they were a bully. A BULLY. Wow, the entire time I had thought that I was the problem and that every attack was my fault. I wasn't losing it, I was quite normal, they had simply been hammering away at me for far too long, gaslighting me every time I spoke up or questioned what they were doing.

Whether you see some of your own experiences in the list below or not, know that gaslighting exists. It's something that took me almost 20 years to see but my hope, dear Sister, is that by sharing a little of my experience you will see it in your life for what it is. Here where some of my symptoms; look and check if any are reminiscent of feelings you have in your own life:

\#   I physically felt like I was losing my sanity or falling through the sky with nothing to catch me; fast accelerating down a numb, emotional abyss with no control.

\# The other person made me feel confused, calling into question everything I said and did towards them myself and the world, making me question who I was and my ability to read a situation for what it was; distrusting myself, my voice and experience.

\# I was constantly apologising for everything, even for things I clearly knew were not my fault, and they would dismiss every apology making me leech onto them for approval, love and validation.

\# I wondered constantly if I was good enough and a good person in all areas of my life and in every relationship, personal and professional. I would hold back from being fully myself in situations for fear of others not being able to take me and therefore drifting away from me.

\# I felt like they were 'normal' and I was the one who needed 'fixing,' taking everything they said verbatim. I started living my life according to the expectations of others even though it made me incredibly unhappy and I began to lie to avoid interactions with them where I knew they would put me down.

\# I was constantly making excuses for their behaviour, saying I was the problem and they were right. I took on their narratives for me and labelled myself as a bad person thinking I was being overly sensitive and emotional, perceiving it as a weakness and the cause of all my pain.

\# I was having the same conversation with them over and over again and because I couldn't convince them or get them to acknowledge my point of view. I started to feel like I was 'losing' it, like I was spinning out of control and that I was losing my grip on reality, questioning everything I thought, felt, said and did.

When I hear the term now, it makes me think of someone throwing a lighted match into a gas–filled room and blowing it up in one big freaking explosion. This is the image that comes to my mind because that is essentially what happens to our soul: it blows up and ends your light in one gigantic explosion.

# #

Gaslighting is when someone uses psychological and emotional manipulation to make you question your memory, experience, perceptions and reality. Put simply, your sanity.

#ColourFULL

The person deliberately engages in this tactic to compromise your psychological and cultural safety, trying to gain more power by weakening your psychological resilience and making you question your sanity. There is no better way to conquer a city than to destroy it from the inside out. Divide and conquer. It's been a common weaponised strategy in the history of colonisation, dividing the mind from the human experience to conquer and malign.

Be aware of what gaslighting and systemic discrimination sounds and looks like

You may have heard some of these gaslighting examples or experienced some of these creeping, discriminatory systemic behaviours play out in the media or around the office:

What it sounds like

\#   I'm not being racist – you're being overly sensitive.

\#   You are taking it too personally.

\#   That's not what I said.

\#   You're reading into this too much.

\#   You need to stop taking what I say so seriously.

\#   You can't take a joke.

\#   I was kidding, why are you getting upset?

\#   You're overreacting.

\#   You're being too sensitive.

\#   You always take things the wrong way.

\#   I didn't say that.

\# You're being emotional

\# If you think that, what does that say about you?

\# You are making it up all in your head.

\# Don't you remember? We had discussed this.

\# If you were listening...

\# If you remembered...

\# Why are you being stupid?

\# This is the problem with you...

\# Why are you being difficult?

\# If you were paying attention you would have heard...

\# What's wrong with you – why do you have to think like that?

\# Why do you always do that?

\# Something is wrong in your head.

What it looks like

\# Ridiculing and making remarks as they pass you.

\# Not letting you speak in meetings or asking you for your contribution.

\# Ridiculing you in meetings or in public.

\# Mobbing (enlisting the support of others to also bully you).

\# Saying that they had emailed you but it must have been 'lost' in cyberspace.

\# Deliberately taking credit for your work.

\# Making jokes about how 'stupid,' 'difficult' or 'incompetent' you are.

\# Taking work away from you because you are not 'qualified.'

\# Discouraging you to not go for opportunities because you 'won't get it.'

\# Deliberately leaving out key information in conversations.

\# Not inviting you to key meetings.

\# Repeatedly giving you the office housework even though you have three degrees.

\#   Treating you and talking down to you as if you were 'bottom of the pile' even though you are equal to them in rank.

\#   Making decisions on your behalf without your consultation.

\#   Constantly speaking and treating you in a way as if you did not understand English or lack skills.

\#   Performance managing you around an area or giving you feedback on a skill/job area for which you clearly have proof that you are highly competent.

And the list goes on. These interactions can be tiring and wear us down and we go in survival mode. This is exactly what the oppressor wants. As Toni Morrison says, 'The function, the very serious function of racism is distraction. It keeps you from doing your work. It keeps you explaining, over and over again, your reason for being. Somebody says you have no language and you spend 20 years proving that you do. Somebody says your head isn't shaped properly so you have scientists working on the fact that it is. Somebody says you have no art, so you dredge that up. Somebody says you have no kingdoms, so you dredge that up. None of this is necessary. There will always be one more thing.' (Toni Morrison, *Black Studies Center public dialogue*, 1975). Gaslighting plays out in all areas of our life resulting in us shrinking our presence and voice and playing small. We hide from attention and people and keep our heads glued to our work. Well-meaning friends and aunties may suggest you do this, keep your head down or shut up entirely, to make themselves feel better about doing or having done the same. Understand that this has been their response but it doesn't have to be yours.

# #

It's important to forge relationships with those who don't continue to diminish your light but seek to spark your fire.

#ColourFULL

Find active allies and fellow sisters who back you when you speak up and out against gaslighting and when you create healthy boundaries in and out of the workplace in the name of self–preservation. A supportive system and community of Women of Colour and allies is one of the biggest ways you can counteract these attacks and their effects.

Remember to always protect yourself from gaslighting attempts both covert and overt and to set time aside to intentionally and deeply reflect. When you do you create an empowering opportunity to glean invaluable insights to heal, reclaim, self–preserve and amplify your personal power, help you protect yourself and other sister in the future as well as refine and tighten your revolution strategy as you press on in your leadership quest and take you and your career to the next level. Reflection builds and flexes your anti–fragility muscles and inner fitness preparing you for an extraordinary and fulfilling leadership experience. When you truly understand and respect your value and are fully convicted of it, you don't need to convince anyone and neither do their words have power on you. Protect your sovereignty and reflect.

*Share the quotes in this chapter with others
so that they too can be elevated, empowered and inspired.*

*Remember to tag Winitha so that we can reshare
your post with our global community.*
Turn to p274 for Winitha's social media handles.

17

Beating the system: awareness and strategy

"When you can't find someone to follow, you have to find a way to lead by example."

~ Roxanne Gay

Sister, let's cut to the chase and to the strategies and tools that you need to beat the system at its own game and advance in your career. With that said, I feel that no intro is needed for this chapter, however, what I will say is that, although awareness is everything and a vital and crucial step in our journey towards equity and leadership, true success begins and ends with action, and that's the only step that counts. If awareness is where the journey begins then action is what will take you to your destination. Commit to action.

Strategise, armour up and prepare for battle

To beat the system, these are some of the things we can do:

\#   Educate yourself on what systemic discrimination and racism is and how it may show up in your life and or career.

\#   Stay away from oppressors, gaslighters and racists. Put down your boundaries firmly, even if they are family, friends or managers.

\#   Feel ALL your feelings. Acknowledge and accept your emotion for what it is. Shout, scream, thump a pillow. Growing up in a culture where showing emotions were seen as weak and dramatic, I found this really hard at first, but when I finally gave myself permission, oh dear lord, did it feel good! Now I don't care what my neighbours think, I give my inner self permission to LET IT OUT and HEAL, BABY! Reclaim that power, voice, truth and identity.

\#   In these situations where we may be questioning our reality, get outside of your head. Go to someone you trust and respect to give you feedback. Reach out to another trusted Woman of Colour with lived experience or a Woman of Colour psychologist for support before you possibly fall prey to the trap of psychological manipulation. Sometimes in the process it starts subtly and it can take a while to understand what is going on. This is why it's vitally important to always share our experiences with others we trust and respect, openly and vulnerable.

If in your gut it didn't feel right, then you are probably right. If you are second guessing yourself then I'd suggest go with your first emotion – it's where the intuitive truth lies. Break down the situation for what it is and go with your gut.

Refuse to let the words of gaslighters, racists, oppressors infiltrate your soul and diminish your light. You are not alone in the world. Call on the power of your ancestors into the room, into your heart, mind and soul and command that they take over your emotions and thoughts. There is a power beyond us, whether it's your ancestors, the Universe or God – call on it and ask that they take over, heal and shelter you, build you up and remind you of who you are: a powerful and magical Woman of Colour who is an exceptionally powerful leader.

When you are triggered by a situation it is an indication to us that our soul still needs time and work to heal. Take the time to prioritise your own healing through whatever method works best for you.

Take the necessary steps: put in a formal complaint, diarise and document that shit. I am talking about dates, times, places, people and the exact words and actions done to you. I recommend documenting everything. Treat it like a crime scene because it is – a crime, a violation against your light and your truth.

\#   Know when it's time to leave. I stayed in a role way too long and I
     ended up with chronic fatigue that took three years to recover from.
     It was intense. Take a lesson from my book; know when you need to
     leave and don't allow their toxicity to infiltrate you because once it
     seeps in, it's hard to get out and it will set you 100 steps back. We
     can't change people unless they choose to change themselves, and
     it is not our responsibility to take on their experiences, emotions
     and or behaviours, to rescue them from themselves, change them or
     to convince them that we are in the right. So, know when to quit in
     the name of self–preservation and self–respect and focus on what
     you can control as well as your personal power and healing.

\#   Keep that strong community of Women of Colour around you:
     mentors, coaches, allies, advisers, psychologists, aunties, mothers,
     grandmothers, sisters to help identify discrimination in its premature
     stages, challenge and hold you accountable and keep your eye fixed
     on the big vision of your life. We don't have to carry ourselves all the
     time. This is why a network of support is so important; you don't
     have to do it alone and neither are we wired to as humans, we are
     wired for connection and to be a part of a tribe for survival. We are
     here for you, dear Sister.

Don't feel bad or sorry for yourself if you don't speak up or speak out in
those situations. Those emotions of fear, shame and guilt will only seek to
hold you even further back and this is exactly what the oppressor wants – to
divide and conquer. They want to divide your truth and power from you to
conquer and oppress you. You are learning and this takes time. Give yourself
some grace. Do what you need to do to counteract their attacks. Walk around
with the 'spiritual army' of deities you believe in and or your ancestors and

those that truly love you. Sometimes, I imagine I am walking inside a bubble so I am continuously protected.

When it comes to speaking out one thing that I have realised is that some battles are worth fighting and some are not. I decided to fight back in the role I had where I was experiencing sexual harassment, bullying and extreme gaslighting by a manager because I saw it was important to take back my voice both in that situation and previous trauma where I had felt my voice had been silenced. Importantly though, I did it so that he wouldn't do this to other women and Women of Colour. To do or say nothing felt like another act of violence towards myself and my sisters. It was an exhausting journey but I could rely on a mentor I had who I called on almost a daily basis for support. I had to ask myself the tough questions to make my choice: do I want to stay or leave and why; and do I have the emotional bandwidth to stay and fight and keep my personal power intact? I decided to stay and fight it out, it was the thing I needed to do to reclaim my voice and my personal power. I came out on top, but I also came out bruised and wounded from an emotional and mentally draining battle. So, my advice is this: if you do want to battle it out, ensure that you have a solid support system and network around and that you have already done considerable work on your personal power, inner confidence and importantly the healing of past trauma. Whether it's a formal complaint, a resignation stating the reasons why, or a face–to–face conversation with the person causing the harm, first talk it through with a mentor or psychologist, it's important to speak it out and get it out of your head with someone that has the experience and or professional expertise to help you. The biggest way you diminish their power is by not diminishing your own. Don't give your pearls to pigs. Beat the system by refusing to yield to it and turn instead to the intensity of your light and its depth, breadth and beauty.

Supremacy, privilege and systemic discrimination

Supremacy, fragility, privilege, dismantling and decolonisation, systemic discrimination, anti–racism – insert 'White' before most of them and you'll have some of the basic terminology you need to armour yourself with on your leadership journey. There is a lot more! Google is your friend. Dismantling and decolonising systems that discriminate against us as Women of Colour is a field of research in itself. It is important to note that the root of this terminology has been created from social and political abstractions and, it can be argued, that this language has stemmed from colonisation; language that has been created to discriminate, suppress, oppress, repress and isolate us. Divide and conquer. On the other hand, it can be used as a resource – language that explains and conveys our lived experiences and those of the dominant culture enabling us to have the conversations we need to have to do the work we need to do as allies and Women of Colour. In my internal and external communication, I try my best to limit the use of the words White, White privilege, White supremacy and so on.

# #

Every time I use them, these concepts cement into my conscious, unconscious and subconscious psyche that I am part of the 'minority' and that I am powerless when, the statistical truth is, the perceived 'minority' are fast becoming the majority; meaning we, in fact, have the power.

#ColourFULL

It is also disenfranchising to say that we do not have any power and are therefore powerless against White people and their systems; that they have all the 'power' and that they are indeed the 'supreme' so therefore we are not.

The best way to suppress us is by dividing us from mainstream culture and making and labelling us the 'minority' and 'powerless.' It's what a wolf does to a little lamb or a lion does to the deer. They work hard to divide it from the pack and isolate it before attacking. But if it stays with the pack, the predator is outnumbered and is unlikely to succeed. This is where knowing who your true allies are is important. True allies are people who have partnered with you to fight for your cause, with you and for you. They let you take the lead and walk side by side with you in your leadership and career journey. We'll come back to how to identify allies in a later chapter. I believe that one of the ways we can contribute (if we so wish) to dismantling and decolonising the system is by partnering with the very people that are holding up the establishment and these structures. We strategically partner with them to use their privilege and so-called power to bring these structures down while uplifting and empowering us at the same time. These are what you call true active allies.

Unite and conquer

By interacting with these individuals (allies) who have joined our 'pack,' we can fence off some parameters to begin this work; we let them know what the boundaries are. Providing a psychological and culturally safe space for them to do this work is necessary in order to get them on board as truly effective allies. We need to breathe as they make mistakes, get it wrong, get up again and keep doing the work because only they can and we need them to. Because here is the truth: they did not choose to be born White just as we did not choose to be born a Woman of Colour. They did not choose to inherit the beliefs and the failings of their ancestors just as we did not choose to inherit the trauma and psychological shackles of ours. We are simply two sets of human beings trying to make sense of the world. Thinking about things in this context helps build the needed empathy to create space for each other to do the work they need to do as together we move towards equity and equality. These allies are the brave few and these are the ones we must strategically partner with. You will need to keep your bullshit radar on and only share some of your emotional bandwidth with those that have the right heart intention, who have the skills to create safe spaces for us and who genuinely want to unite as an active ally with us.

But who is doing the heavy lifting? And, are they?

Dismantling systemic discrimination is not our responsibility unless (like myself) you see it as a mission or career choice you would like to take on. It's the responsibility of all White people. Letting them do this work on their own is like letting a baby pig out into a large paddock on its own; it starts squealing and running around in circles – total chaos. It needs to be given a smaller pen and contained for direction, structure and focus. There are many times where even I have needed to take deep breaths and ground myself in working with corporate organisations and allies because this process is challenging and sometimes downright ugly. As someone with lived experience and expertise in this space, I can see clearly the areas that need to be addressed to provide us with equity and equality to advance and succeed in the world. I can acknowledge that most businesses and individuals are operating from this space unconsciously, consciously and subconsciously. Some may have done academic and or theoretical learning but internal change takes years. I personally have found that having a conversation has been more impactful than what they learn from books and academia because it forces them to look someone like me in the eyes and have that uncomfortable conversation right then and there; to lean in and sit in the fear, shame, guilt or whatever feelings may be coming up for them; to sit in my energy, to acknowledge and to apologise on behalf of themselves, their community and their ancestors. In a way, they are focused to unpack their privilege and dismantle their own thoughts by staring into the face of someone that has been directly impacted by their dominant systems and culture and yet be guided safely by an expert and thought leader in this space to ensure they are not superficially unpacking their privilege and that they are doing the deep work needed. When I feel boundaries are crossed, I reinstate them back in clearly and firmly and decide when I need to opt out of the experience for my own self-preservation and healing. But their learning is not truly learned unless it has been practiced, and there is so much debilitating anxiety around practicing for fear of getting it wrong and being labelled a racist that they are so scared of failure many don't ever try.

It's important that their work is guided and directed by our voices and our experiences and that we are the ones leading and overseeing the work but it is never 100% our responsibility; it is up to them to be the worker bees and us to be the leader. It is always up to them to do the work and the heavy lifting to serve, not save, us. Our role is to lead; to bring awareness, point out the defects and areas that need to be dismantled and decolonised, maybe even explain how it could be dismantled; to show the way and overlook the process, providing advice, feedback and accountability from lived experience. We must lead the work, not do the work. We are the ones with the lived experience but there are few of us who have the emotional bandwidth to create safe spaces for White people to do the work necessary to decolonise, dismantle and provide equity and equality for Women of Colour in particular for First Nations and African and Black sisters.

The oppressors will continue to seek to take, put down, push down and suppress. Sister, we must continue to 'rise up,' as Maya Angelou said, day in and day out. To some of us it may simply mean taking the time to heal and for self-care. Self-preservation is the primary, bare minimum we need to be doing to beat the system. Prove that their efforts are futile by having a united front in this as Women of Colour and start to wear them down and weaken the system at its core. It might not be this generation but if we pass this down to the next generation and equip them with the tools and strategies to self-preserve and heal; if we put on a united front and remain untarnished, unweathered and unmoved and pass this strength on, I am confident that over time this will beat the system and our next generation might be the ones to witness the dismantling of it. For our survival, we cannot at any time be distracted or wavered by any tactic, in any shape or form. That's why having a mentor, coach and community of Women of Colour sisters is so necessary in order to do this. They hold us accountable, challenge us when we make excuses or justifications, cheer us on when we are struggling, help us heal when we are wounded and fill our cup when we are starting to run dry.

\#

Amplify your voice, own your experience and leverage it.

#ColourFULL

Shine your own true light

I believe that one of the most powerful ways we can beat the oppression of the system is by refusing to diminish our light, under any circumstances. If you are not being valued or acknowledged at work then take action:

\#   Nominate yourself for awards.

\#   Speak at events and to the media.

\#   Write and create content on LinkedIn.

\#   Set up a www.yourname.com and publish your expertise there.

\# Set up a Facebook page or create an event or initiative where you can lead a community.

\# Network like your life depended on it.

\# Write and publish a book.

\# Start a YouTube channel.

\# Sign up for the course, not just to level up your skills, but to access a network.

\# Communicate your achievements to the people that have the power to provide you with leadership opportunities.

\# Sit on a board, committee and or volunteer.

\# Get visible, get visible, get visible!

Of course, these take up time and sometimes we have none (although being the coach that I am, I would challenge you on this) and we are simply too damn tired. But do something to brighten your light because it is an important piece in taking the time to understand and unearth the evidence of your own identity, truth and personal power. I am not sure we ever fully know who we are as we are constantly evolving and uncovering our identity, but I do wonder if the real journey in life is to discover the truth of yourself. For the brave few who do this work, there is a freedom and internal peace and joy that is experienced when you understand the truth of who you are and who you were created to be. I often look at those of us who live in Western countries, eat Western food with Western cutlery and dress, act, talk, behave and live in Western ways – what part of our identity has been lost or gained?

Sometimes it's the little changes that are the most meaningful. I once went to lunch at a Sri Lankan restaurant with an Indian and an Indonesian friend. When the food was served, they picked up their forks and so did I instinctively. I then looked and saw a sink close by and I knew that was there because patrons ate with their hands. I looked at my friends and asked them, 'What the hell are we doing? We all eat with our hands and this food is meant to be eaten with your hands.' I got up, washed my hands and started eating and they followed suit. We smiled nervously because there is sometimes shame around the fact that we 'eat with our hands' like it's barbaric or something, some screwed up ancestral belief but I remember it being such a freeing moment. Patrons walked in, some White, some not and I felt proud. This is who I was; this is how I ate at home and I was no longer ashamed about the fact that I ate with my hands that I did so in public in broad daylight. Whatever it is for you, understand the false narratives around your behaviours and work against them. These are the things that all add up and deny us of our experience and our identity, our truth of who we are.

Identity can be what you choose it to be.

#ColourFULL

Take the best parts, the parts that work for you and own it, leave the rest. If you want to eat with cutlery because you don't want the turmeric to stain your nails, that's cool too but take the time and give yourself the chance to understand who YOU are. Choose to live in all your glory.

You were not a mistake. The colour of your skin, your talents and gifts were given to you to be used to uplift, empower, lead and transform the human race. To serve others. You were given purpose and passion for a reason. You were not born deficient. Know that you have the power and ability to succeed and prosper. You have the power to beat the system and overcome the odds if you so choose. I know it is easy to say this, I don't deny it, and as an expert in this space I most definitely know that we can't ever achieve true equity and equality without those with so–called 'power' dismantling the very systems that seek to hold us back and diminish our value and light in the world. But as a fellow Woman of Colour, I also know our past doesn't have to be our reality or dictate it and that in actuality we are the ones with the power.

Let us stand collectively in solidarity and choose to believe that we have what it takes, that we can do it and that we have the power. United we train and build our psychological, emotional, spiritual and intellectual fitness. United we create awareness, strategise and execute masterfully to beat the system. United we heal and reclaim our power. United we elevate and empower each other, charge forward and go forth as a collective, united front. We can beat the system together. It's time for a revolution. Unite and conquer.

Share the quotes in this chapter with others
so that they too can be elevated, empowered and inspired.

Remember to tag Winitha so that we can reshare
your post with our global community.
Turn to p274 for Winitha's social media handles.

18

Networks and relationships: leverage and amplify

"I had to make my own living and my own opportunity. But I made it! Don't sit down and wait for the opportunities to come. Get up and make them."

~ Madam C.J. Walker

We all have networks but often we don't see them. I speak from experience when I say that there are three degrees, or less, of separation. There truly are. I've had too many crazy moments not to believe this truth. However, in my coaching, mentoring and leadership and business training programs, Women of Colour will often tell me that they don't have networks, struggle to create and maintain them and or believe that they just won't be able to access them period because of systemic and structural discrimination. I used to believe this too. I find that this comes from a place of internalised suppression and the fact that, unlike White people, we are aware that we don't grow up with and or have access to the same kinds of networks they do and, in some cases, we are intentionally prevented and blocked from accessing them. In the workplace, we watch as our White colleagues move and shake their way up and around the organisation and create external networks that produce amazing career progression opportunities while we struggle to barely get our foot through the door. As Women of Colour, where we need to start is with a deep dive into our existing contacts and that of our sisters to leverage, expand and amplify what we currently have and from there start putting out threads and building our networks like a spider's web. My advice in this section looks at both sides of the table: reaching out to people to add to your network and pulling back from unsolicited attention from selfish agents to refine and curate your network. I know what gets attention and what gets ignored. Let's dive into three key contexts where you can create and grow your network to amplify and support your wider mission.

LinkedIn

It's a strange beast and I am a daily user of it. LinkedIn has been pivotal in my career. It has created exposure for my work, put me in contact with some powerful people and enabled me to create great friendships with people I have met there. There are a few key strategic things you can do to maximise its potential:

Ensure your profile speaks clearly to your key audience

I came across a profile on a dating website once that compelled me to reach out. Instead of the typical, 'I'm looking for this, I need that, I want this,' this guy's profile was, 'Hey, this is what I'll do for you: I'll rub your feet when you're tired, I'll make you a tea before you go to bed...' Everything in this guy's profile was about what he would do for his prospective mate as opposed to what he was looking, needing and wanting. I instantly realised that this was...true marketing. Whether you are on LinkedIn looking for a job or to promote your business, do it from the perspective of what you can do for them and how you can change their life. Do it elegantly and cleanly and with honesty and integrity. Be fully sold to yourself, convicted in your product or service and its ability to help someone else. Confidence goes a long way and gives you the fuel you need. Don't promise anything you can't fulfil; under promise and over deliver.

If you are looking for a job make sure your Linked picture, description and headliner say so. Check that your profile speaks to the outcomes you achieved in each of your previous roles and quantify it; saying you 'Demonstrated great customer service' is different to 'Increased customer satisfaction by 20% in a three-month period through a commitment to great customer service.' Use the 'what's in it for me' model and focus on value – what value do you provide to employers interested in hiring you? A profile for someone that is 'looking for opportunities' is different to someone who has their own practice or business. Continually adjust and use LinkedIn accordingly. I am not a fan of profiles that desperately scream 'I want to sell you something!' Instead, I focus on stating and demonstrating my value, on selling cleanly and elegantly with integrity and self-conviction while showing up to serve.

Be an active participant in the feed

In the beginning I used LinkedIn passively, liking what appeared in my thread and accepting those that contacted me. Now, I am a little bit savvier.

You've got to post consistently, LinkedIn favours those that hop on regularly. Comment on people's posts, don't just tap 'like' but use it as an opportunity to demonstrate your expertise. You never know who is reading the comments section. People use LinkedIn like Facebook – they scroll. Getting a like or comment exposes your content to their networks and creates that domino effect. If you want eyeballs, focus on posts as opposed to articles. If you want social proof and credibility, focus on articles but know that people are generally lazy to read them unless they want to. More popular are the snappy 150–500–word articles because they allow people to get the gist and leave. People are time poor; I get higher levels of engagement from articles condensed into posts that people can read in full as they appear in their network feed and it has an accompanying image that always grabs their attention. Be strategic and choose efforts that get the most eyeballs in return for your time and energy. Stay in touch with your audience and network to understand what's important to them: what are they struggling with; what are they talking about? Create your content to solve a problem and write, record and post about it. If you are looking for a job, understand what your prospective employers are saying, sharing and posting about. Is there a problem in their organisation and or sector that you think you can solve? Write and post about it. Make your content meaningful, relevant and consistent.

If you want to do video content then know that people prefer videos recorded on a phone rather than of professional quality. I think this is because people want to feel like they are dealing with a human being and not being sold something and having their attention commoditised. People also prefer short videos. I know this dude that films videos that are always less than 30 seconds! Rather than ramble, he tightens up his message and delivers it clearly, simply and to the point. People love it and they go viral. I aspire to be like him one day but, unfortunately, God gave me the gift of the gab. My current record is 8.5 hours of straight talking...

Cultivate and curate your network

As I started appearing more regularly in other people's feeds, I started getting more connection requests and noticed that the majority were from men, a few were people wanting to sell me products and services and about five per cent were genuine and meaningful connection requests. I know some people whose networks are so highly curated they won't accept any request from an individual that they haven't met in person. I'm a little more liberal than that but I do guard my network and don't accept just any request, now I check people's profiles to see who and what we have in common. For introductions with integrity, ask people you know to make one introduction to someone they think you should know.

# #

> Rather than asking them to introduce you to anyone and everyone, the one contact request demonstrates how little time and effort is involved rather than the vague approach which gives the impression of a lot of work.
>
> #### #ColourFULL

This is how we start to build our networks out like a spider's web. When meeting or engaging with people online ask them, 'Is there anyone in your network that could support me with X? If so, I would love a quick introduction via email if you have a spare 5 minutes.' Make your request clear and succinct.

When you do start building a sizeable network don't get trapped in the overwhelm of staying in contact with all 1497 of them all the time. The ones that are meant to be will shine through. Keep in contact with them and focus on building lasting relationships by investing your time and energy in those who show up and add value to your world. Actively grow your network. Search for people in your sector and send them a connection request with a note. When they accept don't go straight in for the ask. Genuinely connect with everyone you meet, give them a chance to get to know you and for them to warm up to you first. Also, take time to get to genuinely get to know them and their world. People want to be engaged with. Share some content with them, invite them to a conversation or event, send them a freebie. If you've met someone at an event you can reach out after and say that you'd like to personally get to know them and that you'd love to hear their views on an article or piece of content that you shared recently. At virtual events you can share the link to your LinkedIn profile via the chat box and invite people to connect with you. Alternatively, you can view the list of participants and add people. My rule and motto for expanding your network is to give before you get. The most meaningful relationships are when you give without the intention of getting. If you give abundantly without the expectation of receiving, you will receive. But first you must give freely. I have some sisters in my network who have been incredibly generous with me with no intention of getting and I know this, I can feel it. However, when they do ask, I will bend over backwards for them. This applies even more as you start to network with high net–worth individuals, senior executives and those with a public profile.

If you want to sell, then my advice is to be explicit about it from the very beginning. Offer support unattached to any outcome. Be upfront, explicit and clear about what you want to provide them and be genuine and honest about what they can expect in return. No one likes surprises and when you have a hunch that someone is helping, communicating or meeting up for a coffee with you just as colleagues and then you get sold to, you can't help but feel a little used. And that is never a nice feeling. Network with respect and generosity.

Events

Be brave, be yourself. I've had a lot of feedback from Women of Colour who have said that they are tired of being the 'only' at events and I get it. It can feel daunting to walk into a room and feel like there are eyeballs staring at you with judgement. These feelings and triggers stem from our internalised suppression. My encouragement is to always go to events with other Women of Colour, if you really want to go to the event then take others with you – there is safety in numbers. I am big on Women of Colour showing up. The oppressor wants to silence us and put us in a box so we are not seen, heard or valued. Every time we show up, we are not just taking a stand for ourselves but also our sisters. So, don't wait for representation of Women of Colour at events; go, attend and represent yourself. Get visible! Put your hand up to speak during question–and–answer time, help out, be a speaker, facilitate or chair a conversation. As Michelle Obama said in her Netflix documentary Becoming, 'We can't afford to wait for the world to be equal to start feeling seen. We're far from it, just time will not allow it. It's not going to happen with one president or one vote, so you've got to find the tools within yourself to feel visible and to be heard and to use your voice.'

If you are feeling bold and brash then go to events alone. I'm a little prideful sometimes when I go to events that I know are 99.99% White. I think, 'Oh yeah baby, keep looking at this face. You're going to see it on a billboard one day!' I leverage that attention to my benefit. If my emotional response is to hide then I ensure that I do what is needed to counteract that emotion because I know it stems from my internalised suppression and past trauma. The best way to heal and override that neural pathway with a new belief and mindset that is going to be helpful (and not harmful like the former) is by taking action, massive action and doing the thing that scares you. No matter how self–conscious I am feeling, I make sure I sit front and centre because I may just give much needed inspiration and support to another Woman of Colour in that space or my networks. We can't let our life and career orbit around fear, it's the act and outcome that is so much more important than the fear itself. Be brave, my Sister, and remember that even though courage and fear go hand in hand you can choose what you pay more attention to and to keep as your focus. Trust your intuition and don't sit at the back of the room. You've done nothing wrong and nothing is wrong with you. You deserve to be seen so sit centre front and be seen.

I ran a Women of Colour event once and there was one sister who had her pitch ready. She went around the entire room, saying her pitch before abruptly handing over her business card and walking off before you could say anything. It was a jarring and shocking experience. A more elegant way to approach the pitch would be to warm people up first. Introduce yourself, ask them questions and be genuinely interested in what they have to say; offer them little pearls of your wisdom and exchange business cards or digital contact cards. After the event, contact them to say how much you enjoyed their company, send them an article or e–book and ask for their feedback and let them know that you would like to connect again. After a few exchanges invite them to be a client.

Again, if you are connecting with the intention of selling a product of service then my advice is to be explicit from the get–go. No one likes a surprise. I once gave my Sunday, my day off, to meet up with a sister. She didn't ask me to be a client or promote her business explicitly but with the questions she asked me I knew that this wasn't a casual Sunday catchup as friends – this was a sales meeting. I felt horrible afterwards, grimy and greasy. The time I gave her was time I couldn't ever get back. If you are going to events to network and sell, my advice is to do it cleanly and truthfully. We don't need to follow western and masculine ways of marketing and selling. We can choose to play a different game.

Go to events with your sisters but don't neglect to work the room. You're not obligated to stay with the same posse, you are entitled to network.

#ColourFULL

Approaching people, particularly groups of people is never a smooth sailing experience. It's kind of like your first day of school. Everyone including you is awkward. It's why going with people to events helps but my suggestion is that once you are all comfortable, split up and work the room. Don't stay in your comfort zone of sticking with the friends you know or that you came with, or immediately attach yourself to the hips of the few People of Colour in the room. Network and show people your brilliance. Far too many times I've made the mistake of getting stuck in a conversation and because I didn't want to appear rude, I missed out on approaching someone else who I really wanted to get to know. Now I say, 'I've really enjoyed this conversation, I'm going to network around the room. It's been great chatting and I look forward to staying in contact.' Approaching people feels really awkward for nearly everyone so I just surrender to the awkwardness and sit in it. I go up to people with a large grin on my face and shimmy my way into their conversation circle. If someone is talking, I'll just nod my head in which case they eventually stop, say hi and ask my name. From there I can then introduce myself, say something like, 'I hope you don't mind me joining. I'm keen to get to know brilliant people like yourselves.' I have also been known to go up to people and gently tap them on the shoulder and give them a huge wave. Be genuinely interested in the people you talk to and what they have to say. If the energy doesn't serve you or they're an idiot, then leave. Trust your inner intuition when you meet people at events. If a remark was made that was discriminatory, call it out with love and respect regardless of if you have only known them for five minutes – you are entitled to speaking your truth and in having your voice being heard. Claim and take your power back in that moment and after, heal. If the conversation doesn't serve you, pardon yourself and leave. If you need air or space to ground yourself, go outside or go to the bathroom. Somewhere where people can't bother you. However, above all, trust your intuition in who you approach because the more you tap into that energy the stronger it speaks to you directing you to invaluable connections.

Keep in contact with people that you met. Business cards mostly gather dust in people's bags. I prefer to text them my contact card so all they need to do is add it to their address book. I do the heavy lifting and ask for their mobile number and then text them on the spot. Another simple way is adding people on LinkedIn straight away. That way they keep up to date with your work, as you post you are constantly popping up in their mind and world and vice versa. Relationships go both ways so if you are getting hardly anything or nothing from them then don't bother, they are not in your camp. Don't waste your time on people who are not going to show up in your life and add value. Set and maintain clear boundaries and if they aren't going to give you much when you contact them, drop it and move on unless you think they are worth investing your time and energy into.

Showing up at events is time consuming and sometimes can give little or no return for your time and money but as someone that goes to events and has built a fantastic network, we can't be using this excuse as a reason to deny us our growth and potential opportunities. And we can't just go to them, hide at the back, speak to those we already know or only hang around our posse or other People of Colour and expect results. When I hear Women of Colour complaining about the lack of representation and not showing up because of it, I tell them that it's the chicken and the egg dilemma. Be the representation you want to see, don't wait for someone else to pave the way, life is too short. Sometimes when you don't 'see it,' you need to 'be it' first so that others can 'see it.' They say that 70% of jobs are found through the hidden job market; employers tapping people they know on the shoulder or scouting for prospective employees through their networks. Not attending events and not networking at events keeps us stuck and from accessing these potential career progression opportunities. These events are also opportunities to recruit allies and potential sponsors; people who can support us in our career or business. Using the excuse of not wanting to be the 'only' and withholding ourselves from attending events or networking only holds us back not White folk. As Women of Colour, when we don't network or put ourselves forward at events and towards meeting people at events, we silence our own voice, value and our presence.

Putting ourselves out there feels powerful and this sinks into our conscious, unconscious and subconscious mind, the decision to choose to take on a new belief that heals and reclaims our personal power and strengthens new neural pathways in our brain, making it easier and easier the more we do it. We also make a powerful declaration that Women of Colour will not be suppressed. So Girl, turn up at the event and if it's a virtual event, put your camera on. The world needs to see your glorious face and that simple act tells them and importantly yourself that the only person who has the right to say if you can or can't enter a space/network, let alone be seen, heard and valued is you. Fight against playing small and push back against the system. Sister, be seen. It's time to get visible!

How to build your network and professional relationships with authenticity

Time as a commodity

I remember a point in my life where I was getting heaps of messages from Women of Colour who I didn't know; some I had sent a message to months earlier to no reply but then randomly I would get a reply with a request for a coffee catchup or a question like, 'How do I start a not–for–profit?' Others would just go in cold with a direct request to pick my brain or get help on something. I said yes to everyone before realising the mistake I was making: I wasn't truly valuing my time. What people don't know is that when you get requests like this persistently and across multiple platforms it is huge tax on your energy, time and expertise. As much as your work is about serving, you start feeling a little used and abused. You start asking, 'What about me?' This applies to creating relationships and networks in general: you want to be courted first, you want to feel valued. Once I experienced this, I understood why I hadn't gotten messages back from some high–flying people who I pridefully thought should have contacted me back. I now knew what it felt like to have people you don't know pull on you constantly without taking out the time to first give, get to know you or 'date' you first.

I once reached out to a contact asking her to be my mentor and made the mistake of asking her to coffee, thinking that the $3.80 coffee that I would pay for would make her feel appreciated. Her time costs $2 000 per hour and what I wasn't aware of at the time was that I was asking her to do this for essentially $3.80 per hour. She replied back with something along the lines of that she was way too busy to have tea with her sister, let alone me, so she preferred to answer any questions over email and not have a structured approach to mentoring. It wasn't until a year later when I was also up to my ears in work and had people pulling on me left right and centre, that I remembered that moment.

When you develop expertise and some level of success you start attracting people that want a piece of what you have and not everyone has good intentions.

#ColourFULL

Most people want to take and it's a horrible feeling; people who feel entitled to just pull at you whenever they so choose and just take what you have spent hours and years to develop. There was a moment when I considered quitting this work for this exact reason – imagine that!

Don't get your knickers in a knot if they don't respond; think about if that was you. You don't know what is going on in their world or what it is like to be on the other side of the table where you are getting bombarded everyday with messages from random people wanting a slice of you, of your time, advice, support and whatever else. Remember building networks is simply a numbers game. Most won't respond or stick around for the long term and that's ok. People are in your life for a season and a reason. Keep showing up with respect, integrity, honesty and love for yourself and others and the universe will reward you. When someone asks me to meet up for coffee or a meeting, I now push back and ask people what they 'Want to support with.' Sometimes the sell that they were planning to ambush me with comes straight out, or they ask me their question and I spend a few minutes giving advice that will change their world. Others don't respond at all and it's these people (and the sales peeps) that I am weeding out with this tactic – those that were never going to do anything with your advice in the first place; the time wasters.

Your time is the most precious commodity you have and when you think about that, it asks you to first reflect on how you are spending other people's time. First impressions count and I cannot believe the number of times I have had to ask people to send me a calendar invite. Instead of meeting up with people to get what you want and then ghosting them, build relationships with them over time. Network really does equal net-worth.

Building relationships with integrity

In this journey I have learned some really hard lessons in valuing people's time and in the process have felt a little bashful about times I haven't done this in the past. I have since changed. If you have a solid relationship and rapport with someone then be bold to ask them for advice, but in that initial contact state clearly what your question is and give a couple of lines of context (not your life story). If they need more context, they will ask. If there's someone you want to speak to who isn't a solid contact, then message and ask them if they have the time and energy to give you advice, ask your question and what their rate is. Tell them that you value and respect their time and expertise. Most people won't charge and I think that's because it's so rare for people to acknowledge and respect the monetary value of your time that when someone does you tend to say 'Don't worry about it, buddy!' The ones that do reply with a cost, you can then decide if it's something you can proceed with, if not then abort the mission. With my mentor, I realised that every hour I took from her, she was essentially losing the $2 000 that she would normally charge a client, or the ability to use that hour to secure a sale worth even more. Now, her choice is her choice but the least I can do is respect her time by asking her what her rate is. I let people know my hourly rate but I also have structured ways in which I can give Women of Colour pro bono support or a more affordable rate through my training programs, workshops and webinars, virtual tea initiative, online and face to face events, social media content, WhatsApp groups, replying to messages whenever I can and this book! This little acknowledgment of others' time value prevents burning bridges and cultivates healthy and lasting relationships with people in your network. The world is small and you never know who you may bump into in the future. Remember, first impressions last. Not everyone charges $2 000 per hour, many will however, charge a non–commercial rate because we know that 'paying people pay attention' and so charging something for our time is simply an act of respect between us both – if you pay for the time, you're more likely to make active use of it and if not, we have been compensated for our time. It also keeps us accountable in ensuring our time with you is going to create real value, impact and results for your career as opposed to meeting up casually for coffee. If you can't afford it and really want their support then let them know that and let them make up their own minds. People value honesty.

Be authentic, be yourself and be interested in others as a person. As Maya Angelou said, 'At the end of the day people won't remember what you said or did, they will remember how you made them feel.' Value yourself and others, be willing to give first and act with integrity and watch your network and net–worth bloom.

Share the quotes in this chapter with others
so that they too can be elevated, empowered and inspired.

Remember to tag Winitha so that we can reshare
your post with our global community.
Turn to p274 for Winitha's social media handles.

19

True allies: how to identify and connect with them

"Don't waste what is holy on people who are unholy. Don't throw your pearls to pigs! They will trample the pearls, then turn and attack you."

~ Matthew 7:6, NLT

Performative allyship is an act of superficiality and I know firsthand how degrading, disempowering and downright idiotic it is. I once contacted someone who was a publicly self-professed ally for 'culturally diverse women' and respectfully and politely asked her for her thoughts on the term 'Women of Colour'. Her reply was a barrage of aggression; her actions gave me the tangible evidence I needed to see her for who she truly was – a fake, an imitation ally. Time is the most precious commodity you have in your life right now. Don't waste it on superficial performers trying to gild their online profile with tokenistic platitudes. Be careful of those who profess to be allies but who haven't done the hard, challenging and difficult work required to unpack their privilege first.

Like you, I've had my fair share of experiences with time-wasters and fake allies. We need true allies to walk alongside us side by side; equality can't happen without us strategically partnering together with us leading the way and lighting the path. Be careful who you let into your life, don't give anyone a free pass just because they appear to be an ally. True power is in deciding whom you let into your life and only choosing to play ball with people of authenticity. They have the potential to harm or help you, disempower or empower you, suppress, or respect you. Dig deep and trust your inner intuition to decipher their real intentional self. Just because they flood their socials with support for Black, Brown and People of Colour doesn't mean they are true allies.

Actions speak louder than words, true allies do the work and show up consistently with heart.

#ColourFULL

They empower you to lead, they follow your lead, are directed by your voice and lived experiences as to what action to take as a true active ally and let their actions do the talking. So, trust your gut, your inner wisdom will know when you meet a real true ally and if their actions and intention are pure and honest. Trust it, protect yourself and find those special few who are willing to walk alongside you to make meaningful change.

Share the quotes in this chapter with others
so that they too can be elevated, empowered and inspired.

Remember to tag Winitha so that we can reshare
your post with our global community.
Turn to p274 for Winitha's social media handles.

20

How to invest in yourself: with insight

"I am not lucky. You know what I am? I am smart, I am talented, I take advantage of the opportunities that come my way and I work really, really hard. Don't call me lucky. Call me a badass."

~ Shonda Rhimes, Year of Yes: How to Dance it Out, Stand in the Sun and Be Your Own Person

When we think of assets, we usually think first about our car, house, technology and cash in the bank. We work tirelessly to purchase these external assets and maintain them. Often, as Women of Colour we are so busy taking care of our families here and overseas, friends, colleagues, basically anyone and everyone except ourselves. I have got a small and modest house. I own one table cloth and three different sets of bed linen; it's minimalistic and everything is from IKEA. I have a lovely car, it's definitely no BMW but it is more luxurious than what some others have. I often think about money and how we spend it and on what. And this idea hit home when I decided to make a really big purchase and invest – in myself.

I've had many one–on–one conversations with Women of Colour who are stuck, stagnant, lost, confused and frustrated. Even when I invite some of them to do my LevelUP program or join The Hustle Club for a very accessible fee their response is, 'It's not the right time; I have to work it out on my own; I'm waiting for my boss to say yes and pay for me to attend' and the list goes on. These are programs by Women of Colour for Women of Colour. Programs that work if you work them to get you unstuck, clear, focused and moving to achieving results and your goals. But frankly, as valid as these excuses may be, what I'm hearing is a lot of them and I'm not seeing a lot of strategic action. Sis, how badly do you want to achieve your leadership and career goals? If you are not doing other leadership programs because they are full of White people or too expensive, then what are you doing? Going back to university to get another Masters or an MBA because it's expected and the norm? Don't wait for your manager or organisation to provide you with personal and professional development opportunities. Many businesses won't fork out $250 to send a Woman of Colour to #ColourFULL conference and yet have spent $2500 per person for several senior leaders to do a leadership conference of negligible value; and these are people who are already leaders. Why the hell would they need more leadership training when Women of Colour need it more? So, now you may be thinking, what hope do we have? Sis, loads! Don't wait for people to give you a chance or an opportunity or to open a door. As so many other successful Women of Colour leaders have demonstrated already, create your own.

As Women of Colour, we need to be investing in ourselves. When you invest, do so strategically and consciously to stretch yourself. By playing small, staying in your comfort zone and doing what feels safe, you deny yourself the opportunities that are out there...even if they do happen to be run and filled with a lot of White people. Start investing in yourself by getting a coach or paying for a mentor. Free just doesn't cut it at a deep level as they will always be too busy and won't think too deeply about their advice, but pay them and they will – it keeps them accountable to you. Just because something is not free does not mean you don't do it. Work, save, borrow responsibly and do it. Invest in yourself by doing the right workshops, events and programs, the ones that are tailored to the specific needs and nuances of Women of Colour, ones that fill a skill gap that you need to take you forward or open up an entire new network resulting in career progression opportunities. Don't just do every event or program, be strategic in assessing where your skills and game is at and what the critical gaps are that need to be covered to change the game for you. Invest in those but above all, girl, please, get a Woman of Colour coach. They will change your life.

Energy and emotions are contagious.

#ColourFULL

Surround yourself with successful people and successful programs. Getting yourself unstuck means reaching out to something outside yourself that is going to help pull you out. Try and get unstuck on your own and you'll be forever stuck. Invest in yourself and level up. It's time!

Don't go back to uni and don't waste your time on the free stuff

We spend tens of thousands if not hundreds of thousands of dollars on university degrees, admit it, we're addicted. Stop going to university again and again and again. I am one of those people; I have been to university four times and earned two masters, a bachelor degree and advanced diploma. For me, doing another university program isn't going to cut it. I see Women of Colour do endless courses, programs, degrees and even PhDs. I believe this pursuit of academic recognition is due to 'imposter syndrome' and all that crap that goes in our heads because of the ancestral effects of colonisation, discrimination and its impact on cultural expectations. As Women of Colour, we have been made to believe that we are not enough due to cultural beliefs and systemic and structural discrimination and racism. We do courses in the belief that they will give us all the answers we need to get from A to B and make us feel good enough, deserving, smart enough and qualified giving us external permission to reach for leadership positions and to pursue a career path. This false underlying belief stems from structural and systemic discrimination that also has us thinking and believing that we need to work three times harder and be 10 times more qualified than non–Women of Colour. I sense that we are actually expecting the course to give us the confidence that we are really seeking, to validate that we are enough, and give us a magic pill to achieve our goals; or we are using it as a tool to procrastinate from doing the real work and action that is required to achieve our goal, for fear of success or failure.

Because governments and institutions view us as 'less than,' a 'minority' and people to be helped there are many scholarships for Women of Colour to apply for. I see already smart, clever Women of Colour getting these scholarships and doing one degree or program after another and the years trickle by without them truly advancing in their careers. They become stuck in the scholarship and education cycle. An example is doing a Masters of Entrepreneurship because you have told yourself that you have no idea how to start a business. So, you give tens of thousands of dollars to an institution that is owned, run and managed by majority White people; you are taught and expected to learn in the White way to create and run a business that you are expecting to give you freedom, joy and fulfilment. Ironic, right? Really, what you need to do is find a problem that customers are willing to pay money to solve and do that. THAT is when you truly show you that you are enough. You don't rely on anyone or anything to give that to you except yourself and so you pursue it regardless. Don't let internalised suppression dictate your life. You don't get the time you spend studying back; once it's spent it's gone. Invest your greatest asset, your time, wisely. Get up and make your dream happen.

All the scholarships and free programs, events and workshops are also not going to cut it. They are going to sell you something or it's going to be a pity fest; a program for marginalised people created by White people throwing around their money and who have absolutely no lived experience; an equitable imbalance of power and a classic case of White saviour syndrome. As Women of Colour, when we do these scholarships and free programs, we reinforce to ourselves that we are no better than charity and that we deserve to be pitied upon. Be discerning about these opportunities as you weigh it up next to your bank balance and self–worth. The majority of these programs are not created for true empowerment or from a place or intention of empowerment. We need to start saying no to programs, events and workshops that are just one big pity fest or sale–a–thon. That's not value. Value is what you pay for so do your research and be sure you don't get scammed (in terms of your personal power, time and or cash) even if it's free or a scholarship. The best free programs or scholarships are from people you already trust and respect or people you know who have done it before. I think the smartest thing you can do as a Woman of Colour is to pay for a great qualified coach or highly experienced mentor to work alongside with you one–on–one to achieve your goals and provide you with support, accountability and a framework. Life wasn't meant to be done alone; experts, coaches and mentors are designed to help you so let them, Sis! Paying people pay attention. Do the hard, challenging and more difficult things and do the paid programs that bring results whenever you can. Investing in yourself does not mean filling your time up with free stuff, value yourself by also valuing others through paid programs. Programs that aren't created by Women of Colour for Women of Colour often operate from and within Western and White expectations, beliefs and ways of working, which conform you to the White way. These programs don't meet the needs, nuances and lived experiences of Women of Colour, which is why I started creating my own programs for us, designed by us, action and immersive–based programs grounded in years of research on our internal and external barriers and challenges and what is truly going to support, empower and inspire us to advance in our careers, leadership journey and businesses. Before you jump into your next program, webinar or scholarship, check whether it is a program from an organisation, sector or market that is steeped in and perpetuating systemic discrimination and racism. Ask yourself, 'By doing this course am I feeding into their system; by doing this scholarship, am I feeding into the imbalance of power and equity created by well–meaning White folk or by stepping into action am I creating my own personal power of how I choose to show up in the world?'

Don't sell yourself short, level up

Some years ago, I attended a UN Women's International Women's Day fundraising breakfast event. Out of the 800 or so people who attended, from what I could visibly identify, only 10 to 20% of the audience were People of Colour. At a UN Women's event... What I saw was a bunch of White women leading the empowerment of Women of Colour, displaying images of Women of Colour as disempowered, as purely charity cases. It made me feel emotionally overwhelmed and something began to brew in my belly. Sitting near the front I sat thinking, 'Does everyone think that's me and that's my story?' What the audience (and importantly the people the organisation served) needed to see instead, was a Women of Colour leading this work telling our story and future from a place of strength and power, not to hear from another White person who is set out to be our saviour. Moreover, at the event I saw volunteer Women of Colour serving, handing out flyers, doing the registration desk and looking after guests but I didn't see any of them as leaders within UN Women and that angered me. After I left the event, I went to a local café and devoured a chocolate lava cake and returned to dwell on a 12–month leadership course that I had first seen three years ago but still hadn't taken action on. Everything about it resonated with me but it cost $30 000. My original plan was to launch my practice, raise $30 000 in revenue and then do the program in August. I sat on the application in the café for 2 hours before signing up for the even earlier May cohort. My total savings were $30 000 and I had no job or income. I could have put that money against my mortgage, bought a new car or invested it. But I decided to invest that money into me, into my mind my future and my practice. The course is a commercial program, not from a university so the investment felt highly uncomfortable and risky as opposed to the times when I had signed up for a degree via government loan. University has changed dramatically over the past several years and I no longer see it as an asset but a liability. What is emerging is a new kind of education: programs and courses that are based on real–world results and developed by real–world industry experts or thought leaders practicing in their field. The most I had ever paid for a program outside of university was $1500 and that felt like a huge commitment at the time. With the $30 000 leadership program, I signed up for the community more than the curriculum. The people in this program are all movers and shakers that I look up to. About 95% of them are White; the majority of People of Colour in the program are men and a tiny slither are Women of Colour. The way I see it, by entering the program not only can I hold the door open for other Women of Colour but I can also be around privileged White people; people who have access to other people, opportunities, networks and resources that I as a Woman of Colour don't have. Hanging around other people in the exact same situation as me is comforting but it doesn't push me to the next level. When you are surrounded by people that are operating at higher baseline than you, you have no choice but to also operate at that level and in doing so you open doors to an entire new career business and life with exciting possibilities. According to Neale Donald Walsch, 'Life begins at the end of your comfort zone.'

When I signed up for the program I was at an intersection with my career. I was about to launch into my practice full–time. At a spiritual level I knew this was the time but I still felt like a total lunatic for forking out $30 000 for a bunch of what was essentially intellectual property that some dude made up, 12 workshops and an hour of mentoring once every three months. Some of my friends thought I was being kidnapped into some clan or scammed. This was the biggest investment I had ever made on myself. I had no job, no income and had committed all of my savings to the program in full faith that it would make a return two to three times on itself. You don't need to be like me and take all your savings and invest it into a commercial program. I have developed a high tolerance for risk and have a deep spiritual connection to God which guides me. I don't advise you to take all your savings and dump it into any program but I do ask that you invest something into yourself strategically, deeply and intentionally. I could have decided not to sign up, thinking that the leadership program was another form of White supremacy and dominance (White people trying to tell me how to be a leader and run my practice and life). I could have decided not to sign up, thinking I didn't want to be the only Woman of Colour in the room again. I could have argued that they were another White club that prevented People of Colour from accessing a better life because their programs did not have a solid focus on equity, diversity and inclusion from the inside out. I could have argued that the price of the program kept People of Colour out, that they should be providing us with scholarships and that this was another demonstration of privilege, power and supremacy by White people. However, I didn't. I know that my greatest asset is myself so I focused my attention there rather than thinking about all the negatives I could pick out to talk myself out of it.

So, was signing up for the program worth it? Absolutely. I made six figures in my first six months and received referrals to potential clients from inside the community who also ended up being quite supportive and encouraging of me and my racial equity work. So why did I sign up and take that initial risk?

We need more Women of Colour leaders who are commercially successful and independent, to look up to and to support and lead us, not more White saviours.

#ColourFULL

I knew deep in my soul that that person had to be me and that if that was what I also preached through my work then I needed to first role model it myself. At the Women's Day breakfast, I could hear God tugging and pulling away at my heart. I knew that I needed the program and that trying to get myself unstuck on my own was not an option and neither would it work. In order to 'see it, to be it' I had to first 'be it,' blazing a path forward and upwards for my fellow sisters.

Women of Colour need more women to look up to beyond than Michelle Obama, Oprah and Beyonce. We need Women of Colour who are from a wide range of ethnic backgrounds and who are succeeding on a level and in a way that is meaningful for them. It's going to take a long time for systemic discrimination and racism to end and for organisations to treat Women of Colour with equity, equality and justice. It's the harder, longer more difficult road but what I know for sure is that the women who have broken through the double–triple glass ceiling, the one thing they all have in common is that they didn't wait. They went out and got what they deserved and wanted. If you want to level up then, Sis, don't wait. Invest in your greatest asset, you. It will give you the biggest returns on your life, career and business. Enrol in that leadership program, get and pay for a qualified and experienced Woman of Colour coach and mentor to work with you and go to those events. Remember, you don't get your time back, spend it wisely and choose to stand in your personal power by going directly after your dreams. Don't waste money on university qualifications unless you absolutely need them. Invest in nuanced programs tailored to the unique needs and lived experiences of Women of Colour and lastly, please don't use education and training as a form of procrastination from doing the thing you really need to do to achieve your goals. Your future self will thank you. Know that you are already enough; you are clever enough, smart enough, skilled enough, experienced enough and intellectual enough. So, take the right kind of action, the kind of action that will propel you into who you truly are; powerful you.

*Share the quotes in this chapter with others
so that they too can be elevated, empowered and inspired.*

*Remember to tag Winitha so that we can reshare
your post with our global community.*
Turn to p274 for Winitha's social media handles.

21

Your A team:
plug in to accelerate

"I believe that telling our stories, first to ourselves and then to one another and the world, is a revolutionary act. It is an act that can be met with hostility, exclusion, and violence. It can also lead to love, understanding, transcendence, and community."

~ Janet Mock, Redefining Realness

The ongoing joke with Women of Colour in my community is that we are always doing more than one thing at once. We're not just a career woman, we're an author, entrepreneur, speaker, daughter, sister and friend. We always have more than one iron in the fire and are often supporting everyone around us. It's also very common for us to have 3–4 side hustles, businesses or career paths on the go while working, studying and doing life. I often wonder if this is us being ambitious or if it's us feeling like we have to overcompensate to succeed and to be truly valued, seen and heard in the world because we are a Woman of Colour. I think this is one of the things that actually holds our potential and progress back, that we are seeking success, validation and fulfilment in all spaces. In an attempt to diversify and prove ourselves all things to all people, we create an additional layer of inequity and an imbalance of power for ourselves and in the process become dispersed and diluted.

I believe we spread ourselves thin like this because we have been suppressed for so long. Our potential has been a flood of water held back by a dam of oppression, and so we go into overdrive to break the banks by starting several businesses, projects, initiatives, career paths and side hustles. In an attempt to get at least one foot into the door we operate from survival mode, furiously trying everything we can possibly think of in order to not just survive but to 'make it' and thrive. We get hooked by the newfound sense of freedom that comes with starting initiatives, doing more study, switching and or pursuing multiple career paths and running several businesses – a freedom that we wouldn't encounter if we just stuck to one 9–5 job. The downfall of this diversification and newfound sense of freedom is that, when it comes to day–to–day activities, we have become unfocused and burned out. In the pursuit of success, leadership and career growth, we sign up to all the free workshops and leadership programs, go to all the events and work hard at our businesses. We are scurrying around like rabbits doing this and that, bouncing here and there and anything and everything that moves either scares us or gets our attention. The result of this frenzied but unfocused effort is that we don't have much to show for it despite working hard and wearing ourselves out. Our brand and potential get diluted, we are busy but not really doing or achieving substantial results and our precious time is lost. We sacrifice a part of ourselves in the quest for success as we, in the process, fight back against the external oppressors and to free ourselves from our own internal suppression.

There is no issue with being multi-passionate but if you want to get ahead in life and build a successful career then we need to be thinking more strategically and simplifying.

#ColourFULL

We need to get very clear on who we are and the difference that we want to make in the world. It might be helpful to think about it backwards: what impact and difference do you want to make and what is that one thing you can do right now to enable that? Then work forwards by doing that one thing and then do the next one thing, and the next...one day, one action, one step at a time. I have thought very deeply about this because I myself have been that dispersed and distracted person and there is a part of me that is still that person. What I have learned over time is that there is value in having a sharp and narrow focus. We should aim to first become the master of something and be known for our mastery so that we can then position ourselves to leverage it and transition to the next thing. Over a period of time, you will hone and sharpen your skills and develop a portfolio as evidence of your professional skills, value and worth. This is a much more effective strategy than trying to throw one ball at several targets at once. It also comes down to knowing yourself. I know that a diversity of tasks makes me perform better, I've tested this and know that I need to do more than one project to really stay engaged in anything. If I take on more than six projects then my performance starts slowing down. It's a fine balancing act and one that requires you to know yourself and to seek and employ external, expert support. So, unless you too know that you require diversity in your work to stay engaged and be a high performer, my advice to you is to think long and hard about why you are doing several things at once. If you are finding it hard to let go then I would look for the one thing, the most important thing for you right now, and allow the other things become more a side hustle and background to your primary focus.

The key to keeping us focused and clear among the chaos of life is people we can depend on however, it's our hesitation in this space that prevents us from reaching out for and accepting support. There are some of us that think that we're fine on our own and that it's ok to stay where we are in our comfort zone; we can figure it out or maybe we don't deserve to be helped and supported because reaching out for support may make us look weak and we can only depend on ourselves to make it happen. However, one of the most powerful things you can do to create and maintain clarity and a sharp focus (internally and externally) is to seek help. Going deep within ourselves and tapping into our internal self can help us drive our leadership and career goals, situations, decisions or business forward. However, what will take you to the next level and support you to become a high-performance leader, are external resources that will also help you to get clarity on what is happening in the marketplace, with competitors or within the workplace.

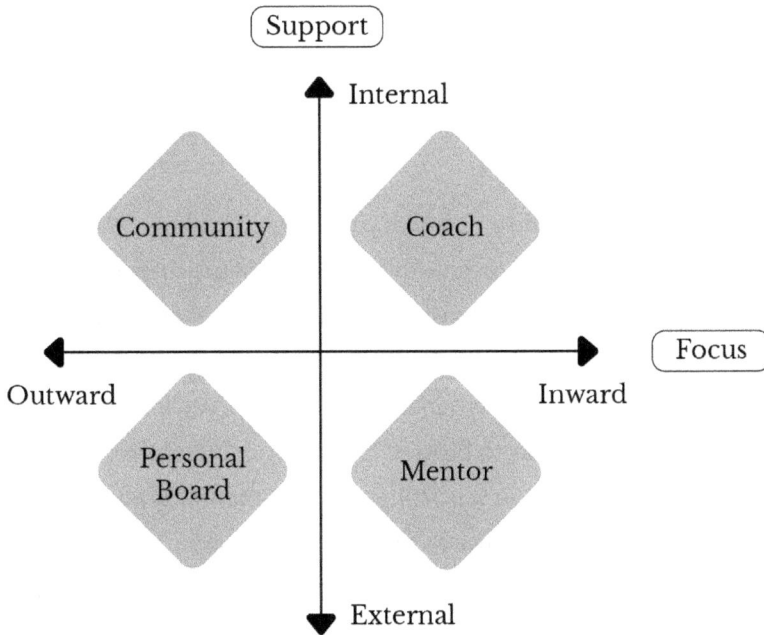

Build your A team with the acceleration model

The way I work through this with my students and clients is with the acceleration model, a tool I have designed specifically for Women of Colour based on my research. This model will accelerate your career and give you needed support by plugging into four important areas. Support is crucial to guiding your focus, and gives you clarity and a competitive edge that's leveraged and amplified; this can be found in the form of a coach, a mentor, a personal board of directors and community.

Coach

A qualified, trained and experienced life/career/executive/business coach will support you to find out what is going on with you at a deeper level. Their focus with you is inwards to your internal self. They might help you find out what you truly want in life and work with you to unpack what's holding you back. They work with you to dig in deep and to pull wisdom from within to give you the answers you need to keep on track to achieving your goals.

Mentor

A mentor is someone who works with you to support what is going on with you internally with a focus on how this is driving, influencing and impacting what is happening externally to you. Say you wanted a leadership role, they might give you feedback on your resume, run mock interviews with you, advise on how to land that promotion and which skills you may need to work on, recommend networks to build or support you to determine your next move in line with what you want for your life. A mentor gives you specific advice based on their expertise and experience to support you to navigate the world and its external events so that you stay focused and on track to achieving your goals. Stick to office hours or the hours they work when communicating with a mentor to be respectful of their time and energy. With emails, texts and face–to–face or virtual catchups, be respectful and conscious of their time. If possible, always try and seek Woman of Colour mentors, these are the most effective kind of mentors for us; people who know the journey, have forged a path for us, battled our battles and can give us nuanced and tailored advice specific to our needs, desires and lived experience. They also create safe spaces for us to be truly vulnerable and enable us to see it so we can be it; a constant reminder during the tough times that we can achieve, be successful and become transformational leaders.

A mentor–mentee relationship is a coveted one. Successful mentor–mentee relationships require trust and respect from both individuals, towards themselves and towards one another. I don't believe that we truly know how to trust and respect others if we don't trust and respect ourselves first. When we don't that's when we risk jeopardising others' cultural and psychological safety. The best mentor relationships are where both individuals are healed and have worked through their internalised suppression. If either party has deep wounds from trauma that are still raw or run deep and if neither individual has healed then this risks the safety of the other and the relationship becomes dysfunctional and toxic. If this is the case for you, I suggest seeking out and engaging with a

A suitable mentor is someone who you have chemistry with, a rapport and a fast and deep connection.

#ColourFULL

professional, qualified Woman of Colour therapist before engaging a mentor. A good mentor will point this out as you start to engage with them and gently request that you seek support through a therapist first before working with them. Although tears may come from sharing a difficult or traumatic situation, a mentor is not a replacement for psychological and emotional support and help. It is our responsibility to take care of our emotional and mental health and to not dump it on them regardless of how 'close' we may be with them. They can hear you and offer some kind of support but their role is not to help you heal or overcome trauma, and to expect to engage them in this is unethical and unprofessional.

The mentor–mentee relationship can be formal with paid, high level structured support, or informal with a casual catchup here and there and phone calls and emails when advice is needed. I suggest you negotiate the terms with your mentor. If they can't give you the level of support you feel you need, thank them for their time and find someone who can. But if there is someone who you greatly admire and can learn from then I suggest working around their requirements – meet them in a way that works for them, as frequently as they want and see fit. The best mentors are also the ones that you pay for, when you pay for a mentor there is skin in the game for both of you. It makes them show up in a different way and makes you show up in how you perform and what you do with their advice. Paying for their time also ensures that you get access to them consistently and for suitable periods, for example my Women of Colour mentees through the LevelUP program have one-on-one, hour-long, fortnightly sessions with me and receive consistent online support, accountability, strategies, tools, templates and resources in between sessions including emergency sessions if needed. If you are not paying for your mentor then, at the bare minimum and even if they do not expect it, stick to the time limit and pay for lunch. Show your appreciation by handwriting a nice card or giving a small gift; a little gesture goes a long way for what is the investment of their time and energy into you that they don't get back.

Respect your mentor's time and energy by implementing their advice and working hard at your goals. I cannot state enough how demotivating it is for mentors when they spend all this time and energy on you and you remain stagnant because you have done nothing and chosen to do nothing. We are engaged in and energised by your progress and commitment. We understand, as Women of Colour ourselves, the stagnation you may be experiencing from systemic barriers, but if you are not putting in the elbow grease then there is no point us being your mentor. And at the end of the day, a mentor cannot make you automatically succeed, they are not a magician. Their job is to give you advice from their experiences which may work for you and may also not work for you. It's up to you to decide if you want to take it and implement it or not and to let them know either way. Respecting a mentor's time is also about implementing their suggestions or at least giving it a go. If you don't feel their ideas are right for you, your career or business then speak up and explain why so they are aware and do not waste time and energy continuing that path of advice. Speak this out respectfully with love and grace. When you trust and respect your mentor, you put in the work and keep them updated on your progress.

Having more than one mentor might be great but it can also be confusing if and when you receive conflicting advice. If you are going to have more than one mentor then separate them for the different facets of your career, business and or life. I have a mentor for my thought practice over all, one that mentors my intellectual thinking and another that is a mentor for my spiritual life. Mentors can be for a session, months or years. It is also not unusual to 'outgrow' your mentor; I have experienced this many times and it's exactly what great mentors want to see, to see you rise to their level and beyond. When this happens, celebrate the end of the relationship with a lovely meal or ritual and find a new mentor that will continue to stretch and grow you.

As someone who has created mentoring programs and mentored many people over the last 22 years, I can say that it's ok if it doesn't work out but when it does, it's truly beautiful. There is nothing more incredible than witnessing another Woman of Colour who you've been mentoring blossom, thrive and fulfil their biggest potential. So, get yourself a Woman of Colour mentor, someone who has walked through the trenches and knows exactly what it's like to be in your shoes, to help you navigate your career and future success. The best place to find mentors, besides LinkedIn, is at Women of Colour events. Take your business cards, network the rooms and utilise the strategies in chapter 18. A mentor is one of the most powerful tools you can claim in your leadership toolkit.

Personal board of directors

A personal board of directors will keep you focused on the path to achieve your goals. This is similar in concept to a board of directors for a traditional company except they don't own you nor are they 'shareholders' of your career or business. Their job is to provide advice and support as to the direction and growth of your career. They consist of people who you trust and respect; an outward looking lens that sees what your goals are, the work, the networks, resources and contacts needed to make it happen and they provide you with guidance and support to grow and avoid potential pitfalls. They look at things strategically, challenge you and hold you accountable. For me, a personal board of directors not only includes my top allies, sponsor, mentor and coach but also includes people who inspire me by keeping company with them. Someone can be successful in an area, but they can also be a real jerk. Keep company with people that inspire you, not jerks. My personal board of directors also includes what I call 'cheerleaders.' I think of them as my diehard fans that come to every game. These are my friends, professionals who get what I am doing, believe in me and keep me on track when I show signs of veering off, wanting to come to a complete halt or reversing and going back to my comfort zone. They remind me why I am doing what I am doing and what I want to achieve, and push, provoke, challenge and hold me accountable until I get back on track. Sometimes they even pull the covers and drag me out of bed (so to speak) and give me a gentle loving kick up the booty. They constantly remind you that the world needs you and all you have to offer it.

A community of Women of Colour

One of the reasons why I went with the term Women of Colour in this book, instead of focusing on one particular ethnic group or my own, is because I saw that we operated in silos. As someone who is a bit of chameleon and easily adaptable, I knew the value of coming together but I also saw the racism and discrimination that exists in and across our cultures due to internalised suppression and learned behaviour and beliefs from colonisation. I heard the struggle of some sisters feeling 'too White for Black people and too Black for White people;' I saw sisters being isolated by their families and communities for being 'mixed;' sisters being put down by other sisters for being too pretty; for getting that job or not getting that job because of their skin tone; sisters suggesting to other sisters that they lighten their beautiful skin before their wedding day; the racial slurs at dining tables when families and sisters would talk about Women of Colour from other ethnic groups. All of this and more deeply troubled me. Shouldn't we be unifying to stand in solidarity against systems and structures of oppression? Aren't two threads intertwined stronger than one? This is one of the reasons why I also started doing this work, to bring us together to stand in solidarity through my online and face-to-face events, #ColourFULL conference and awards night, the private membership community, my programs, workshops and initiatives, digital content and now this book. Everything is built around community. The higher intention of all this and future work, is to not just equip Women of Colour to succeed and thrive, but also for us to stand in solidarity as we forge forward in our collective revolution. As Women of Colour, we have a responsibility to advocate and stand for our sisters collectively and their communities as well as be each other's biggest allies, particularly for those that may experience more oppression than us. Rather than operating in silos, we accelerate when we unite and put up a solid front against those that seek to oppress us. Like an army about to walk onto the battlefield, we come together and stand in solidarity, side by side with each other, unmoveable, unshakable and charging forward; leaning on the strength and courage of each other and our collective wisdom, our collective energy. We can do this today by coming together as a community and by being each other's biggest advocates and allies, cheerleaders and supporters.

Women of Colour tend to be the 'only' or one of few in a department, business, organisation, industry or team. We are isolated and it can feel like we are battling the whole world; you against the majority. For this exact reason, we need to be plugged into a community of Women of Colour. By coming back to community, living in community, living for community and giving back to community we return to our true higher self, the essence of who we are and that of our ancestors and people. We don't have to conform to White ideals and beliefs around succeeding through individualism or masculinity, our cultures have been built richly on community.

By creating and staying constantly plugged into a community of Women of Colour, we redefine leadership and lead a unique, feminine, culturally inclusive and safe way to succeed.

#ColourFULL

And we lead it from the front and from our hearts. By coming together as one community we end up succeeding; bringing healing and collective wisdom and leveraging our collective power. This is the gift we bring to the world and THIS is our most powerful strategy and competitive edge in the marketplace and our leadership journey.

Safety for us is not just physical, it's cultural and psychological. Cultural safety is an environment that is safe and free from the violence, challenge, provocation and denial of people's identity and experiences and from racism, discrimination and bias (conscious and unconscious). The dignity of all is upheld through the shared intention to learn and listen as well as have shared respect, meaning and knowledge. It is to have the knowledge and respect for others and how our own bias may affect them (yes, even other People of Colour) and for their cultures and the diversity that exists in those cultures. At a deeper level, it is about the removal of individual, institutional, structural and systemic barriers, biases, racism and discrimination. Similarly, but separately, psychological safety is when there is respect, permission, interest and trust between individuals and people feel safe to be themselves without the fear of negative consequences on their self-image, sense of self, position, career or status (William Kahn, Psychological Conditions of Personal Engagement and Disengagement at Work, 1990). For Women of Colour, it's the ability to bring your whole self, your inner and outer world, to work without the fear that what you think, feel, say or do may result in negative situations towards yourself or withhold you from opportunities. Where we can speak up and out, receive and give feedback, make mistakes, assert ourselves and express an opposing view without fear of being harmed. To me, psychological safety is the opposite of oppression and oppressive environments where we constantly have to pay an emotional and mental tax by continuously playing on the defence. Psychological safety is complete freedom to be yourself unapologetically.

I am sure that while reading the above many of you can think to past or current experiences and events where your cultural and or psychological safety was compromised, where it has become unsafe for you. When we engage in community, we have the utmost obligation to ensure the cultural and psychological safety of our sisters from our own ethnic communities and from others. The things we say or do that stem from our internalised suppression and unhealed wounds have the potential to jeopardise our sisters' sense of safety. That is the opposite of solidarity. Being part of a community, therefore, is consistently doing the learning, unlearning and relearning work within ourselves to ensure that we create safe and nurturing spaces where all are valued, respected, seen and heard for their whole selves. Many of us come from high-context cultures where there is a strong value of collectivism for survival, support and advancement. In modern times and through colonisation and migration many of us have lost this. Some don't even know who their neighbours are. By creating spaces for and tapping into community specifically led by and for Women of Colour, we give ourselves the opportunity to tap back into our ancestral and cultural values and beliefs to lead and to accelerate as opposed to succumbing to Western beliefs of succeeding through individualism and masculinity. To not is a denial of our ancestral knowledge and wisdom, cultural identity and our own identity. I suggest being a part of communities that are made up of Women of Colour who are also ambitious and driven and who have like-minded values, career paths and goals. They will become an external resource that also holds you accountable and challenges you. They also inspire, empower and motivate you to keep you focused. When you surround yourself with like-minded people who all have similar goals and are actively reaching to achieve them, you can't help but want to reach yours too; the shared energy is infectious and a little healthy competition is good to keep us on track and moving.

The key with community is to plug in. Get active, give before you get and contribute consistently and deeply with intention, love and respect. By giving generously with no expectations, we receive everything that community has to offer. What we put in is what we get out. In online communities I've observed that there are those individuals who do what I call a 'dump and run,' blurting out what they need or want to promote and then checking out, and they get little to no engagement. However, those who are active participants and givers in the community do. Give before you get and give your time generously without attachment and the expectation of receiving and with no hidden intention. It's the karma of life to give and live life generously. Make it part of your personal brand. In large communities, member activity is sporadic but the ones that engage consistently are the ones that are known by the community. Regular engagement keeps you at the front of people's minds, tempting them to check you out, and gives you a competitive edge making you stand out from the rest in terms of work ethic, commitment and generosity. Don't just be a bystander, engage actively, offer the hand of support to those that need it and start meaningful conversations in your community. Comment on posts, share opportunities and start provoking conversations; share deep insights and reflections and achievements you want to celebrate, volunteer to help out at events, speak at them. Be an active ambassador and spokesperson for the community. It's also important to show up physically and virtually at Women of Colour events to create and forge new relationships and have a sense of belonging that will ground and centre you. I know in the events that I hold, even just walking into a room (or a virtual room) of hundreds of other Women of Colour is liberating, leaving many attendees buzzing for days. There is nothing quite like the feeling of walking into a room where you are the dominant majority and people look, sound, behave and have had similar experiences to you. It's been healing for Women of Colour to hear from others on the stage and when networking about their experiences in life, leadership journeys, businesses, careers and the workplace.

It's incredibly powerful when your experiences, thoughts and emotions are validated after doubting yourself for years in isolation.

#ColourFULL

By plugging in consistently, virtually and face-to-face, you give yourself the opportunity to empower yourself, energise your batteries and to learn from other Women of Colour who are a few steps ahead of you or have succeeded in their careers.

It is our responsibility to pass the baton. It's like you're running a race, you have got a baton in your hand and your job is to run the sprint as hard and fast as you can, so you can pass the baton on to the next Woman of Colour so that she can pass it onto the next and together, as a team, you win the race. The baton is your success toolkit, your sprint is your community and the road that sprinting is your leadership journey, the path forward you are creating for other sisters. By running as hard and fast as you can you are able to pass on that energy, momentum and competitive advantage to your sister in order that she, too, can pass it on and together, we win. In our careers, business and lives it is our responsibility as a sisterhood, as a community, to pay it forward to each other, advocate for each other, be each other's mentors, coaches, sponsors, allies, cheerleaders, advisers and biggest supporters. To be each other's family. When we get a seat at the table it is our responsibility to hold the door open for other sisters so that they can hold the door open, and another sister can sit down, and another and another. We must not be afraid to reach below to a Woman of Colour and pull them up over and above you, so to speak; to give them a job or opportunity that will see them succeed beyond ourself. There is abundance for all; collaboration over competition, collectivism over individualism and community over isolation. In honour and respect to our ancestors and the sisters that came before us, we have a responsibility to uphold, love, revere, respect, elevate, empower and pay it forward to other Women of Colour. Plug into your A team to accelerate in your leadership journey and pass the baton so that collectively we win the race towards true success, freedom, equity and equality.

Share the quotes in this chapter with others
so that they too can be elevated, empowered and inspired.

Remember to tag Winitha so that we can reshare
your post with our global community.
Turn to p274 for Winitha's social media handles.

22

Conviction:
knowing your value

"We are not born women of color. We become women of color. In order to become women of color, we would need to become fluent in each others' histories, to resist and unlearn an impulse to claim first oppression, most-devastating oppression, one-of-a-kind oppression, defying comparison oppression. We would have to unlearn an impulse that allows mythologies about each other to replace knowing about one another. We would need to cultivate a way of knowing in which we direct our social, cultural, psychic, and spiritually marked attention on each other. We cannot afford to cease yearning for each others' company."

~ M. Jacqui Alexander, Pedagogies of Crossing

When I was about 21, I became an Export Manager. I didn't apply for the job. I was promoted into it and told I was doing it by my boss without being asked. Being the good, Brown girl, I consented and took the promotion even though I didn't want the job. I was absolutely shit scared thinking I couldn't do it and would buckle under pressure and stuff everything up. The only other real job I had up until then was a year and a half as an Export Clerk in the same company. When my boss told me that the salary was $30 000, I very shakily asked him if he could make it $35 000 and he told me to ask him in six-months' time. That came and went and he deferred again, telling me to ask in another six months.

I worked exceptionally hard in that job and went over and beyond what I was expected to do. I churned out documentation so fast my fingers would get swollen. My boss knew and saw how hard I worked, how I had a knack for business and making money and took advantage that I was a timid, young, Brown girl still in university. This is why he had told me I was doing the Export Manager job and didn't ask. What he didn't know was when the previous White Export Manager was still around, I had seen her pay check and knew she was paid $67 000 per annum plus a company mobile phone and fuel card; more than double what he had paid me plus benefits. And this was a Man of Colour too, not some old, White dude. Because I was responsible for my department's profit and loss statement, I could clearly see how much revenue and net profit I had generated compared to the previous Export Manager. On top of this, I saved large multinational corporate clients just over a million dollars in expenses by redesigning their entire supply chain as well as increasing their operational productivity while also growing my department's bottom line. This caused one of the CEOs of a massive global company to email my boss directly to let him know how much he valued me and my incredible customer service. My boss forwarded me this email as a FYI, not as a thanks, and followed it with a meagre $1 500 bonus at Christmas. To even ask for a pay rise in the first instance was such an incredibly hard thing to do, it took everything I had. After three years in the role, and after asking for an increase of pay by $5 000 a year and being asked to wait another six months, I quit. It took me three years to understand that my manager understood my value but didn't value me enough to pay me another five thousand dollars per year to keep me, yet had happily paid the previous White female manager (who hardly did any work, indulged in 100 smoking breaks a day, left early on Fridays, spoke on the phone all day to her friends, and took time off for long 2–3–hour lunch breaks) $67 000 per annum plus benefits. After that job I found myself in Canada. I bluffed my way into interviewing for an Executive Officer position at a large organisation in the accounting industry. At the interview, the recruiter asked me what my salary expectations were, to which I replied $35 000. She looked at me long and hard and said, 'No way, you're worth at least $45 000 – don't settle for less than your value.' That comment really set me aback. Since then, I'll admit that it's been a slow grind for me to learn and believe in my value, particularly now that I essentially charge for it. That initial conversation with the Canadian recruiter set the stone in motion as I progressed in my career to negotiate my salary and terms and to do so with complete integrity, conviction and confidence in myself and the value I bring to people, the team, organisational culture and the business.

What is essential are the skills, expertise and experience to back your claims to add value and ability and confidence to live up to the value that is expected, at the terms you've requested for. If you are in the process of building your skills, experience and expertise then look to the value you can offer in your resourcefulness, aptitude and worth ethic; the strengths in your character, your personal brand. Reputations stick around longer than pay checks or job titles and personality characteristics are the real drivers to achieving results – it's the skills needed for innovation and the future of work. This isn't about Women of Colour having to work harder than anyone else, outperforming, defending their characteristics and work ethic, feeling the pressure to not make mistakes or having to be more; we are clearly overqualified and undercompensated. But as someone that has hired and contracted Women of Colour of varying levels, my invitation is to work with a mentor and or coach to sense–check your value in today's marketplace, your ability to take it to a new level and to regain your self–belief, confidence and conviction – it's highly likely you are undervaluing yourself due to internal and external barriers and challenges, past and present. Sometimes when we go into survival mode, get caught up in an opportunity or haven't reflected enough on our value, monetary worth, expertise and the leadership journey ahead, it backfires and sets us and our confidence back even further.

# #

Getting managers to listen when you ask to be paid your worth or to receive an opportunity or promotion is tough but what does help is the conviction with which you ask.

#ColourFULL

Ask from a place of absolute inner belief and confidence that you not only deserve it, but that there is no one else better than you; that only you and you only have a unique special sauce that is going to change their world and that of the organisation. This conviction is best supported by your A team: the people you trust and respect. When I made the massive jump from being an Executive Officer to being a General Manager (GM), it was because I had a mentor at the time who told me that I could and should be doing GM roles that were $150 000 plus. That figure blew my mind. My lack of self–esteem had kept me in the line of work and salary level of an Executive Officer and to go outside of it felt frightful. That was until my Administrative Assistant had a straight talk to me and told me I could be doing my boss' job. I thought, 'Right, two people have now told me this so I'd better believe, shouldn't I?' I went for it and applied for a GM role after spending a considerable amount of time with my mentor dissecting the position description and matching my value, experience, skills and qualifications to it line by line. This gave me the confidence I needed which gave me deep conviction at the interview. After that exercise I knew I could do it standing on my head, I just needed an opportunity. When I got the job, I exceeded the expectations of the role and in six months had achieved 80% of the KPIs stipulated in my two-year contract. I ended up doing the CEO role and started smashing out the KPIs for that too. One night after a board meeting, the Deputy Chair told me privately that she had no idea why I was working there and that I should be working for some large corporation earning easily over $250 000 with my skills. As she had a HR background, I trusted her and believed it even though I was pretty shocked. She talked through what I had achieved for the organisation and aligned it to other corporate commercial offerings in the market. She helped me to see the bigger picture in terms of my value both in terms of my skills and pay.

After that conversation, I engaged an Executive Coach who'd had a high-flying career in a range of corporate senior positions and who was now a qualified and trained coach. She confirmed this in the first meeting through conversations about my career this far and through a hell of a lot of psychometric testing, each test having over 300 questions! She then gave me a good talking-to as to why I wasn't playing a bigger game career-wise; showing me that my skills were not truly being valued and compensated accordingly. So, I left the company and started applying for CEO and Executive Director roles only to be shocked with the interest and interviews I was getting which emboldened me to make another move up. What I learned in these three big leaps forward in my career was that in order to build confidence I needed a bigger stage to dance on to give me the opportunity to see the evidence of what I could really do. The human mind sometimes needs evidence to support new unfamiliar beliefs (in my case confidence) and faith, to believe without seeing. Having mentors and qualified coaches (my A team), in my corner who had the right experience and expertise supported me to stay grounded and to do what I call a sense–check, for example was the role and salary figure that I have in my head realistic in the marketplace; could I move into that role with where I am at in my career; does my value (my skills, experience and expertise) stack up and match the expectations of the role? The point is, if we just had these conversations with our managers, who want to keep our value for their greedy little selves, we would get nowhere. There is value in pausing. What we need to do is do our own research and seek external advice and counsel from our A team of a personal board of directors, mentors, qualified coaches and community of Women of Colour and allow space for our internal wisdom to speak. When opportunities are thrown our way, you're allowed to say, 'Is it ok if I reflect on this and get back to you by X time tomorrow?' I do this. People will often try and call or email me and ask to pitch to me in person but I now ask everyone to email me. That way it's documented and I have time to pause, reflect and forward to someone else for advice. It also forces the person engaging with me to get clear rather than wasting an hour of my time discussing random things and not delivering a clear pitch with all the detail. I want the moves in my career to be strategic and deeply intentional. To do so requires pausing, reflection and well–thought–out effort as well as engaging in external advice and support to get outside our minds.

Quantify your worth

There are two aspects to quantifying our worth, and by worth I don't mean your self–esteem but your position in the job marketplace. The first is around the framing and the second your monetary compensation or salary expectations. When I was still in university and wanted to get a job, I went straight to the library for a how–to and picked up a book called *Tap into the*

Hidden Job Market. I learned how to adapt my language to make it compelling and evidence–based, for example instead of 'Displayed excellent customer service' I would write 'Secured a seven–figure account in three months through incredible attention to customer service and satisfaction.' Taking the advice and suggestions in that book to change my resume is what ultimately helped me land my initial first job as an Export Clerk which then led to the role as GM and CEO. I even tracked down the author and paid her $60 for a career coaching session and to look over my resume. I was being paid $12.50 per hour at the time so this was a huge investment for me and the very first investment I made into myself and my career (degrees aside of course!) One of the most powerful things I gained from that experience, and have continued to do throughout my career, was the ability to quantify my achievements in order to frame and position my worth in the conversation around my salary from the onset, and to have that documented on paper as a reference tool.

> *As you move from middle management to senior and then onto executive, the need to keep and quantify evidence of your worth becomes more and more important and can form part of your employment contract.*
>
> **#ColourFULL**

I've never left this to the responsibility of anyone except myself. I measure and track the performance metrics that are in my contract, projects, tasks and performance plan. However, the thing that has set me apart is that I've also always tracked things and metrics that are important and valued to the employer in my future ideal role. For example, when I was an Executive Officer, I knew a key area for a GM was financial management. So, I put my hand up to take a few tasks off my manager's desk and threw myself into financial modelling, budgeting, reporting and forecasting. Well beyond the expectations of my role but coveted skills in a GM. I used this to practice and make mistakes, and also to gain the experience and track the outcomes of this work to put that on my resume. As Women of Colour, we often do work that feeds into a pipeline, leaving someone else to take the credit. Make sure that you track and quantify your achievements as well as document any qualitative data you might have, such as testimonials from clients and team members and thank you emails from stakeholders or managers. When applying for new roles for my next career role, I was unashamed in asking the people I trusted, including external stakeholders like suppliers and clients, to write me a testimonial of how brilliant and amazing I was. I told them the roles I was applying for and gave them the specifics as to the skills and experiences that would be valued for those roles. I then injected these testimonials into my cover letter, key selection criteria and interview responses as social proof. As someone who now has their own practice, I still track and measure everything and do not rely or allow clients to set or inform these metrics. This is because I am also tracking the data that is needed to influence the next level in my career and the necessary conversations that will take me there. It informs my confidence in charging a certain monetary amount for my intellectual property and time as well as framing conversations when I pitch this value, so that it has substance and conviction.

I've never relied completely on someone or something external (besides my A team) to tell me my worth or to quantify it for me. I have not relied on performance plans, job descriptions or key performance indicators in executive contracts. This has also been me covering my ass. If you don't own and tell your story, someone else will do it for you and I can guarantee you it will not be the story you want to be told as a powerful Woman of Colour leader. I've spoken to some sisters who have, unfortunately, had people question their performance as a tactic to move them out of the organisation or deter them from applying for a promotion. There is nothing more compelling (or satisfying!) than drawing out a long list of well documented achievements to counteract efforts that attempt to thwart your prosperity. This is also important in performance review meetings, when we are having conversations around progression managers may have reasons that seem to make sense on the surface but are what we know to be total bullshit. Call it out by taking out your folder of testimonials from internal and external stakeholders and a list of your carefully and well documented achievements and results including all your outcomes that have been quantified. If you have applied for an internal promotion and have been denied, use this information as a strategic move to have an assertive conversation about why you didn't get the role and the possible systemic discrimination and racism that may exist in the organisation.

Whether it is a reminder in your calendar once a month or every quarter, take the time to go through your department's and organisation's monthly, quarterly or annual reports for evidence of how your contribution has improved team, departmental and organisational performance. Take the time to strategise your next move or step in your career and ask yourself:

What skills and expertise are most valued in my dream leadership role and what would set me apart from other candidates? How will I build these skills and what data could I track as social proof of these skills and expertise?

What systems do I need to put in place to capture this data?

\#   Who are the right people that need to see this data and information and how will I put it in front of them consistently as well as present it in a compelling way?

\#   How will this differentiate me and make me stand up and out? How does this add to my personal brand and what story can I create around it?

\#   How does this position me strategically for career opportunities and how can I use it to frame the conversations I may need to set up these opportunities?

\#   Where are these conversations being had and with whom and how do I access these spaces and networks with personal power, confidence and conviction?

Take the time and effort to track and quantify the value you bring and document it in your resume and in performance meetings, interviews and job applications. When things are documented there is a weight and substance that is added, it's incredibly powerful. It becomes your reference, the evidence and credibility you need and can depend on to pursue opportunities and counteract any attacks on your professionalism.

Communicate your value

Part of knowing your value is communicating it to others. Most people are caught up in their own lives and roles and they won't all know your brilliance. Relying on others alone to take the time to recognise it disempowers us as Women of Colour. As warrior leaders, we don't leave it to just anyone, we take full control just like an organisation that crafts precise messages that position and reinforce its positioning and branding. When you live and lead from within first, you do not rely on others to dictate your value and or to communicate it to you; you don't look for validation and fulfilment in others. You do this yourself. When we engage in this level of personal branding work, we give ourselves the opportunity to recognise and value ourselves and to tell the story of our own worth and potential, that is 10 times more powerful than others valuing you. When we truly value ourselves, it in turn asks people to value us. When we get visible and communicate it, we give ourselves the air time we need to position ourselves for future opportunities and they have no choice but to listen. In the process we reclaim our power from past situations of discrimination and racism; we give ourselves the opportunity to mend and to heal by recognising our own value and standing firm in the recognition of our worth. In doing so we liberate other Women of Colour around us to also do the same. Tracking and quantifying your value is important for your current and future roles and for your personal brand. When we take the time to proactively and strategically plan when and how we will communicate our value to the audience to support us in taking the next step in our leadership career, it can also prevent those from taking credit for your work. It gives credibility, evidence and substance to your communication efforts that will position your personal brand powerfully. Be proactive and two steps ahead to beat and fight back against the system.

You can communicate your value in other ways beyond the office by building your expertise through the sharing of ideas, deep thoughts and solutions via blogging, LinkedIn articles, contributions to industry communications such as magazines and newsletters and through professional organisations, membership and leadership development organisations and associations that have existing communities and networks. You can also ask to speak on podcasts, host your own or seek out media opportunities by commenting on hot issues or writing opinion pieces as well as speak at events, conferences and run webinars. If you are concerned about how this external activity might impact your job you can put a disclaimer such as, 'These are solely my own views and not those of my employers.' By communicating our thoughts and therefore our values at events, industry conferences initiatives, networking events, programs and other channels, we give ourselves a 'unique selling proposition' that can be adapted to your personal brand; your point of difference that sets you apart from competitors and makes you compelling to prospective employers that might be interested in engaging your services. What is your competitive edge and advantage? This goes for day–to–day conversations at work, events, parties, on social media. When people ask 'What do you do?' what do you say? Communicating your value to the public as opposed to reiterating your job title will support your career progression by increasing your networks and drawing people who want some of your juicy energy into your sphere. It puts you on the map and positions you for your dream leadership role.

When we live from a place where we know our worth, we know what we deserve to get paid, what roles and opportunities we deserve and how we deserve to be treated. We don't put up with nonsense and drama.

#ColourFULL

Live from a place of worth

We set and put in place plans to create the change we want to see in our careers, whether it be having conversations with people, making a complaint to human rights authorities and formally to HR, applying for new roles or leaving a current one. We ask for what we want, need and deserve. We do not allow ourselves to be dictated to by others who are not our true allies as to what should be doing, feeling, saying or being paid. Period. We set in place self–determined plans as contingency strategies such as having three to six months of living expenses stored safely away in case the bullshit at work gets so much that we choose to leave, you need to rebrand or pivot your career or if you realise it's not the job for you. That's personal power. Savings give financial empowerment and freedom to Women of Colour to make powerful, proactive choices in their career, and the time to make and execute strategic moves as opposed to getting stuck living from survival mode. Or sometimes, life happens and we may need to take a sabbatical or unpaid leave from work to tend to our personal life to simply give ourselves time to recuperate from systemic discrimination and racism; the emotional and mental tax we pay as Women of Colour. Time off is self–care and activism, not laziness. Having a contingency plan in place for your life and career is an actionable way to be self–determined and live from a place of value and not leave your life vulnerable and at risk of falling prey to the oppressor; it empowers you to thrive, Sister, not just survive! This is true success for Women of Colour.

The process of uncovering and knowing your value is like finding a rough diamond. Life clouds our sparkle. It's time that we hit pause and take the action needed to polish and cut it to let the brilliance shine forth. Acknowledge, celebrate and communicate your value. Take control of your career direction. Humans are not mind readers, if you have something special to offer to the world and you truly understand and respect the value you bring and if leadership is what you truly want, then lead from the inside out from a place of personal power and, damn it, make sure the world knows, scream it from the mountain tops and cheer for yourself while shaking those pom poms (if that's what it takes).

Share the quotes in this chapter with others
so that they too can be elevated, empowered and inspired.

Remember to tag Winitha so that we can reshare
your post with our global community.
Turn to p274 for Winitha's social media handles.

23

Courage: visibility and personal branding

"Understand: I don't ever want to be equal to any other being. I always want to be greater...in all things, in all circumstances."

~ Brandi L. Bates, Remains To Be Seen

Personal branding done right can open a myriad of opportunities. It goes beyond content, colour, font size and words and definitely beyond fashion. For Women and People of Colour, it's a powerful tool that will help you advance. It has for me and I know it will for you. With the future of work rapidly changing we know that Women and People of Colour are the most affected as we tend to sit in junior to middle management roles. When technology replaces job functions or when something like COVID happens and businesses need or want to make fast cuts, we are generally the first to go. We need to future proof our careers and legacies and stay two steps ahead of the game. Exhausting to some I know, but trust me, a fulfilling and fun way to do this is through a personal brand that excites you! A representation and extension of who you are, something that tells your story and the terms of which you wish to create success and leadership on. Two examples that I look up to as personal branding done well are Misty Copeland and Bozoma Saint John. I have been following both ladies for several years and have seen their social media following, career opportunities and lives thrive as a result of their branding. For Women of Colour, I believe they are the benchmark and what I personally aspire my personal brand to be.

Don't fake it 'til you make it

It is crucial to understand that personal branding is not conforming to the system, oppressors or anyone's views, beliefs or expectations about who you are or who you should be; in fact, it's the complete opposite. Personal branding is about who you truly believe you are. If you are a little unsure how to unpack this, I suggest asking friends that you trust and respect to name three reasons why they are friends with you; push them to give deep answers. It will give you a clue as to which facets of yourself to put forward and incorporate into your personal brand. Beyonce is an example of this: after splitting from her father's management, she went out on her own and dived into who she is. Her music may not have initially been as commercially successful as her past work but it was and continues to be highly creative, unique and powerful and over the years has catapulted her success to a whole new phenomenal level. Great personal branding takes who you are now and amplifies and leverages it to move you to where you aspire to be. Along the way your personal brand will evolve as you do; it's a journey. When you start to think about all the moving parts of what makes you, you, it can get a little overwhelming and confusing trying to thread it all together.

Do not get stuck on who you want or think you should be. Creating a personal brand based on who you wish you were or want to be is disempowering; the denial of self, one's circumstances, experiences, truth and identity, messy bits and all. The fake it 'til you make it approach to personal branding can be destructive for Women of Colour, already far removed from our ancestral roots and disconnected from our cultural identity. Due to colonisation and migration, many of us work, live, think, talk and dress in western ways. Much has been stripped from us so it doesn't make sense to create a brand based on who you think people want and expect to see and to 'fake it,' but instead to create a powerful brand around who you are. In my training, coaching and mentoring work, I often see Women of Colour who in their 30s start questioning who they are and it almost has them in a bit of a tailspin. What I love about Bozoma St John and Misty Copeland is that their cultural identity is physically, intellectually, commercially and visually intertwined into their personal brand through their content, careers and messaging. For Women of Colour, success and career progression is not about stepping into a new you but rather into who you always were: a remarkable woman who was a little buried and suppressed among the effects of racism, systemic discrimination, colonisation, societal and cultural pressures and expectations, pain, suffering and trauma.

# #

Freedom is shedding ourselves of all those layers and coming back to the core of who we are and were always destined to be.

#ColourFULL

This approach to personal branding creates power because, Honey, you are enough! Trust a sister right here.

Bluffing and bragging

As someone who has sat on the other side of the table, I can speak with assurance that our radar picks up when people are bluffing and outright bragging. It makes sense that your personal branding cannot be a bluff or inherently false picture. We are not that person. We are us. Many of us, culturally, do not value self–promotion and it is particularly discouraged if you are a woman; we are expected to follow the systems of the hierarchy and patriarchy. For those that have migrated to or live in western countries, we are expected to be grateful for our lot and speaking up in any way is shunned in the fear that you may rock the boat of the norms that have been established. We fought so hard to get here, please don't ruin this, is what they say indirectly. The journey to assimilate has been hard for many first and second–generation migrants and speaking out means we stand out and can become a target.

Some might argue that to get ahead in the western world we need to stop being 'shy' or hiding our achievements, that we need to put ourselves out there, 'brag' and self–promote. Self–promotion doesn't mean to speak from a place of ego, convey false information or fake it 'til you make it. I strongly believe that it's vitally important for Women of Colour to engage in a healthy amount of self–promotion for visibility, healing and to reclaim oneself towards the building of personal power, success and freedom. However, there is a difference between self–promotion and bragging. Bragging is masculine and White in its approach to succeeding, it promotes individualism as opposed to collectivism and, as Women of Colour who come from collectivist cultures and have had much of our identity stripped away from us, conforming to the system's ways of succeeding only provokes existing wounds and is the continual denial of self. My encouragement is to be self–aware and know when you are self–promoting and when you are bragging and as always, promote your sisters as much as possible the collective. When we thrive, we all thrive and when we all thrive, we thrive. I do understand, however, that for others, masculine approaches to working and succeeding is very much a part of who they are and works for them. We are all different and no one size fits all.

I have a dear friend who is brutally honest in everything she does and says. She told me the other day how she was approached to do some work with a national organisation, a huge financial and career opportunity for her after a long period of struggling to get her business off the ground. Rather than position her consultancy business as something it isn't, she was upfront and honest, told them that she was still new to the whole business thing and asked them what she should invoice them for. Most business books, thought leaders and consultants would suggest that you don't do this but I love that she did. Her big purpose is around truth–telling and I love that she was honest and upfront about it because it showed her values of integrity, honesty and vulnerability and to me this is what her personal brand is about and an alternative perspective to deep and impactful self–promotion. Great news, she booked the client!

Position yourself in the market

Personal branding isn't just about visibility, inherently it's a positioning tool that will help you advance in your career, leadership journey and or business. Positioning is like getting a tattoo: you want to think long and hard before you get it branded to your forehead and removing it can be painful. If you are not sure, get a temporary one and try it out but know this is surface level and in order for it to stick you need to do the deep work to make it permanent. Your personal brand takes who you are right now and uses that to position you to take your career to your goal. Don't be confused. Personal branding is definitely not just about what you wear, social media content, followers or number of likes or shares, your job title or company name. Personal branding done well aligns; it powerfully communicates the essence of who you are and your values attracting leadership, career and commercial opportunities, the clients you love to work with and doing work that gives you freedom, joy and fulfilment. Be authentic and celebrate all the parts of who you are, the parts you love and the parts you love less. Every part of you. Take on an emotionally healthy approach to personal branding and self–promotion that solidifies the foundation of your career and positions you firmly putting you on track to achieve your ideal career or job so that you don't end up in the future looking back wondering, 'Who am I,' 'How did I get here?' and 'Who have I become?' This is your personal power.

True personal branding occurs behind the scenes with relationships and gaining people's trust.

#ColourFULL

Creating relationships

Some will say that it is what people say about you when you are not in the room and what people say when they describe who you are, or that it's not about being known but being known for knowing something. Use your head and heart in union with each other and find meaningful heart–centred ways to connect with people. Connect face to face (virtually or in real life), form relationships and ask for referrals or what you need and want and do it with honesty, generosity and integrity. Greet people and shake their hand, looking them square in the eye, shoulders back, your head held high, standing from a place of personal power; full of confidence, courage and conviction in who you are and the value you bring to this world. Approach people you know and don't know and strike up conversations, contribute your thoughts to publications and digital platforms, create your own and share your ideas and expertise. Create digital resources, videos and downloads, contribute to online conversations, podcasts, webinars, virtual events and discussions, create your own events and bring people together. This also invites and draws people to connect you and form relationships. Connect and converse with people in your field regularly over LinkedIn and other social media platforms. For people who are their own business, show up where your clients are, hang out where they hang out, strike up conversations with them and speak at events they go to. Be intentional with whom and how you form relationships and how you leverage them to feed into and build your personal brand. Do they enhance or pollute your personal brand? Build or destroy it? Amplify it or hold you back? Devalue or value it?

Reputation, trust and credibility

We don't have to play to the White western ways of marketing and self–promotion or lean into toxic masculinity. We can choose to play a different game and create credibility through integrity, honesty and by choosing to do the deep work. It's kind of like beauty companies. There are companies that pump a whole lot of their budget into marketing instead of producing quality products, we buy them and then get deeply disappointed. Then there are the boutique companies that pump their budget into genuinely creating brilliant products that solve a problem and work. They are the ones that go viral; they take a little longer but they don't need marketing because these are the companies that we trust and promote through word of mouth. They are credible and credibility builds personal brands that last and leave a legacy.

The people who don't have the patience and self-respect to build integrity over time are the ones that burn out fast. In my experience, these are the people who struggle financially in their business, leadership and in climbing up the corporate ladder. You may point me to Joe Blow who became an Executive Director by bullshitting his way up and tell me how much more experienced and qualified you are than he. Yes Sis, I know and hear you but you don't have to be him to succeed and, if so, is 'success' on those terms worth it? Is it truly being free? Or is it being captive to systemic and structural discrimination and racism by giving in? These circumstances occur because of systemic discrimination, not because of your lack of personal branding or that you are deficient in the attributes needed for the role. People like him may have somehow gotten to the top but they are, and will always be, remembered for all the wrong things. Their reputations are built around falsehoods and at that level their lack of knowledge, skill and positive attributes are on clear display for the whole world to see. Don't let the system force you into suppression and oppression by being someone that you are not. Beat it by building credibility through integrity, honesty and consistent deep work and succeeding on your terms. A sustaining and strong personal brand that leaves a legacy is one that is built on credibility. So, find your niche, do your homework, form your opinions, become obsessed with it. Emotions and energy are contagious. Be a master of your expertise and you will be remembered for all the things that make you and your ancestors, community, culture and sisters proud.

# #

Build credibility, that to me is true,
timeless personal branding.

#ColourFULL

Confidence and conviction

At the time of writing this book, I have a stack of research on my desk that is almost a metre high, over 500 pieces of content on Evernote, another 350 on a hard drive and a mini–library at home on my book shelves. This does not also include the thousands of content items that I have digested over the past few years, all around the advancement of Women and People of Colour, diversity, inclusion, justice and equity. I have had over 150 one–on–one conversations with Women of Colour, have mentored and coached many more through my programs and connected with thousands around the world via social media, my private online Women of Colour membership community, physical and virtual events and so forth. So, when I talk about Women of Colour, the just words pour out. It's a second language to me and why I can stand in conviction of my confidence as a Thought Leader and expert in this field.

Word goes around fairly quick if you don't know your stuff and, as someone who sits on the other side of the table, it is obvious to see who really knows their stuff and who doesn't. In fact, it's irritating because these people bombard us everywhere. You know them, the people on those YouTube ads with videos taken on their phone reading blandly from a script about how they changed their life became millionaires and will change yours to by signing up to a free webinar. When deep work hasn't been done the person in front of you does not look convicted at all. You can see right through it! What's sad is when I see some Women of Colour opt to play into this. Spend the time doing research and then some more (but put a time limit so you are not using research as a form of procrastination from doing the real work that you are avoiding). The key here is quality over quantity; put stuff out there that is meaningful and deep, don't just do it for the sake of it. Don't be a content generation machine. Be someone that transforms people's lives. Critique your own thinking, form your own opinions about ideas, theories, approaches, strategies, tactics. Don't just digest content assuming that you are busy learning and growing but digest to form your own opinions and stretch your thinking. The audience, stakeholders, your manager and other people can sense and see when you have substance and this radiates through your personal brand. Choose to do deep work consistently, and build confidence and conviction.

Your voice and presence matters

In my work, there seems to be two sets of Women of Colour, the rare few that put their hand up for everything and who are constantly appearing on my social feeds, and those who have something really valuable to share with the world but instead slide to the back of the room and rarely show up on my feed. If representation is important to you then you need to be a part of the solution even if that means being the first in order that other sisters can see it to be it. Not doing so means that you are giving into the oppressors' game. This is not the game we play at the level of warrior leadership. Warrior leaders fight and push back by speaking out, being visible, putting their hand up, sitting at the head of the meeting table, doing the inner healing work, grabbing the opportunities when they do come their way, showing up unapologetically and unashamedly as themselves at all times, sitting front and centre at events and large gatherings, pursuing leadership with grit, elevating the collective and their sisters and stretching themselves and their potential outside their comfort zone. Your voice and presence deserve to be heard, seen and valued. Personal branding is all of this and although it may be challenging for Women of Colour due to inherent systemic oppression, we must resist these forces and persist to succeed on our terms, fighting and pushing back against the system and ultimately beating it at its own game.

People are drawn to brands and people that have something that they want. Confidence and personal power are rare commodities in today's personal branding marketplace. It pays to do the hard, challenging and deep work of facing your own fears and limiting beliefs, freeing yourself from internalised suppression, healing and putting yourself out there in the world unashamedly and unapologetically. To be seen to be heard, be visible. Representation matters. It may feel a little clunky, and uncomfortable at first but, like a muscle when flexed, it becomes easier and stronger.

They are strategic where their words and energy is thrown to hone and align to their positioning. Choose the long game; your past doesn't need to be your present or your future. Leverage the fact that you are a Woman of Colour to advance you and your career forward by owning all of you. It's time to get visible!

Remember, self-promotion and personal branding is simply you communicating yourself to the world. The world is not filled with psychics and mind readers – people don't know what you've done or achieved, your expertise, skills, talents, experiences and qualifications. As authors of our lives, it is our sole responsibility to communicate this clearly, elegantly and simply to them with the intention of advancing our careers and achieving our leadership goals. It is about taking control of the narrative of our own lives, past, present and future and not leaving this to anyone or anything. If we fail to do this, we risk others writing our story for us. Your life is yours to live, dear Sister. Take control of your story and tell it powerfully.

Share the quotes in this chapter with others
so that they too can be elevated, empowered and inspired.

Remember to tag Winitha so that we can reshare
your post with our global community.
Turn to p274 for Winitha's social media handles.

24

Freedom:
thriving in white structures

"Every voice raised against racism chips away at its power. We can't afford to stay silent."

~ Reni Eddo-Lodge, Why I'm No Longer Talking
to White People About Race

My gut feel is that out of all the chapters this is the stuff you want to know the most. There is so much that I wanted to write in this chapter; so much that I want to share with you on how you can thrive in White structures both from my extensive years of deep and intense research, the lessons from my own career and those of other Women of Colour who have been able to get a seat at the proverbial table and succeed in leadership. This chapter could easily be an entire book in itself. To try and fit everything into one single chapter would prove futile and perhaps remiss of the delicacy and tenderness that this topic requires. So, what I've decided to do is to give you the top, simple-to-implement strategies to get you ignited and, you never know, I might write a second book just for you dear Sister, dedicated entirely to thriving in White structures.

This chapter reinforces what we've covered so far and expands on the mindset, tools and strategies needed to navigate White systems and structures while maintaining your sense of identity, personal power and what makes you, you. This chapter does not ask you to act, think or be White and or like a man; to do so would validate and affirm the system and the actions of the oppressor. Neither is this chapter about how all White people are bad; it is not a detailed account of colonisation, feminism, gender, intersectional and critical race theory, or an in-depth analysis and study into how and why these systems were created and how they work and operate to oppress us or how it's White people's responsibility to dismantle individual, systemic, structural and institutional discrimination, racism and White power, privilege and supremacy in order for us to thrive. I'm pretty sure that by picking up this book and reflecting on your own lived experiences you have a pretty clear idea of what the system looks like and how it works to oppress Women of Colour.

\#

Rehashing what the problem is or what's not working only gets us so far, can retraumatise us and deepen our internalised suppression.

#ColourFULL

By picking up this book I know that what you are looking for is the tools, strategies and support to succeed in your leadership journey on your terms despite progress made and the pace of progress on the equity, justice and equality front. In this chapter this is where we bring it all together. This chapter is about solutions and challenging your way of thinking and approach to succeeding in career, business and life. What this chapter is about is how to thrive in and among the chaos of White structures. It's about how to manage and navigate them to create a successful life and a leadership journey that is fulfilling, freeing and energising to you and brings you abundance, joy and peace. As discussed in earlier chapters we know that we need allies we trust and respect to walk alongside with us and having allies is an integral part of our leadership journey that will help unlock success. What I do want for you to do in this journey is to maintain integrity in everything you do and to have a strong sense of self and identity. To do so renders you powerful, it is your resistance and activism towards suppression, oppression and discrimination. We know that the first step in leadership for Women of Colour is in healing. Step two is how we view and perceive White people systems and structures (a powerful key to freeing ourselves from internalised suppression). American novelist, playwright, essayist, poet and activist, James Baldwin, put it perfectly when he said, 'There is no reason for you to try to become like White people and there is no basis whatever for their impertinent assumption that they must accept you. The terrible thing, old buddy, is that you must accept them.

And I mean that very seriously. You must accept them and accept them with love. For these innocent people have no other hope. They are, in effect, still trapped in a history which they do not understand; and until they understand it, they cannot be released from it. They have had to believe for many years, and for innumerable reasons, that black men are inferior to White men. Many of them, indeed, know better, but, as you will discover, people find it very difficult to act on what they know.' (James Baldwin, *The Fire Next Time*, 1963).

Far too often we rush into the exciting stuff, like what we've been working on in Part 2: Rewrite Your Outer World, when where we truly need to start is in Part 1: Reclaim Your Inner World. The foundational truth to thriving in White structures is that the success and leadership we always knew deep down that we could attain are not found in solely knowing how to have difficult conversations with White people or understanding how to play workplace politics. To thrive in White structures is to succeed on our own terms in freedom, and freedom requires us to lead from the inside out. When we are thriving on the inside, the outer world matches what you are experiencing in your inner world. Alignment. True freedom and success are the feelings of joy, peace, laughter, excitement and fulfilment day in, day out as well as financial security. The key to thriving and succeeding despite White people, their systems and structures is in chapters 1–23. Focus on the 23 chapters that came before this one; dive into this work to free your internal self from the psychological shackles of modern–day slavery, to heal and reclaim, amplify and leverage your personal power resulting in the creation of abundance, freedom and wealth. Lead from the inside out; you are the person you need to invest and trust in the most to lead yourself. The hardest leadership gig you will ever have, is the leading of self. Master this and you will be an exceptional leader.

The long game

Being in this world, I know all too well the grind of this work and how complicated it is. It's the long game, ongoing work that is not achieved by a few workshops or in under six months. Reaching equity and equality for Women of Colour is going to take years. Through my thought leadership practice, I work with what I call the bold, brave, courageous few. Organisations that want to do the work to build racial equity. And when I say few...I mean few. Thinking about this can get depressing but know that there are other people like myself and others that are actively advocating for your freedom and doing the deep and intense work within corporate organisations to build inclusive and anti-fragile cultures of allyship and racial equity for Women and People of Colour. The other realisation we need to make is that people won't change unless they choose to change. Even though my training is mind blowingly brilliant (if I must say so myself), if they don't make that internal commitment and decision to change then nothing will change. All the jumping around, fist pumping, activism, advocating and brilliant business case writing in the world won't change them unless they choose to change. Knowing this saves me from slapping myself in perpetual disbelief. This is why I also work on the other side of the road and directly with Women and People of Colour to equip them to succeed, regardless of whether or not these idiots decide to change. If they do then great, we'll take them out of the idiot basket and into our ally basket. If not, let's let them remain forever branded as idiots.

As James Baldwin wrote, allies are going through their own journey. What we expect them to do on our behalf is a massive call for anyone and at the end of the day we are not White and therefore don't truly know their lived experience. However, if we were in their shoes, we might feel the same. From my work with White allies, I do know that they tend to experience a lot of shame and guilt particularly over their ancestral history and biases. If you question this, pick an area of diversity (ageism, disability, LGBITQA+,

First Nations, there are many) in which that you have no lived experience and some discriminative beliefs about and make it your job to be an active ally, or try changing a core belief you've had all your life. Although they are the ones that need to dismantle and decolonise systemic oppression and White supremacy, because it's linked to human behaviour it's going to take a while. People don't change overnight, and being an effective and true ally is a lifelong journey of constant changes to beliefs, mindsets, human behaviours and lots of good, old–fashioned hard work to create systemic change. So, what are we going to do in the meantime? Sitting around and waiting is not going to get you anywhere and, Sister, life is too damn freaking short. Go out and get what you want.

'If they don't give you a seat at the table bring a folding chair.'
~Shirley Chisholm

Don't like the table? Take your chair and go find a new table!
#ColourFULL

It's going to take a while for allies and organisations to do their thing. In the meantime, a much more effective strategy to becoming influential and impactful powerful leaders that transform the world is to learn how to thrive in, manage and navigate White structures, systems and cultures. To do so is our resistance, our activism and our revolution.

Isn't hard work enough?

No. And this is coming from someone who used to pride herself on only sleeping 3–4 hours in her 20s and used to work 50–75 hour weeks for months on end. Working harder will not get you more results. For many Women of Colour, there is a societal, cultural and community expectation and belief that we must work hard because of colonisation and systemic discrimination. For many of us this was the way we were raised. Our parents might have put us in afterschool homework clubs, gotten us tutors and made us learn a bunch of stuff from classical piano to swimming. After school and on weekends, we had chores to do and going to the playground was a luxury. As we got older, some of us may have faced pressure to perform extremely well at school, then at university and now continue to work hard in our career. We've been brought up to believe that hard work is enough; that if you get great grades and finish a double degree in a top university that it is enough to land a well–paying job let alone a job that's enough; that staying in that job for the rest of our lives is enough for people that look and sound like us because that's as good enough it's ever going to get. 'Don't rock the boat' our community whispers to us when they see us proclaim 'It's not enough!' and reach out for more. Or perhaps they loudly declare; 'How dare you think this is not enough when it was good enough if not more than enough for your parents, grandparents and ancestors. Who are you to think you can be somebody in this world, some kind of bigshot? How dare you dream!' And so, we believe that we've got to work two, five, 10 times harder than White folk to survive let alone thrive. To some degree we do because of the reality of the world we live in as Women of Colour, but my question to you is do we need to work harder than White folk to succeed and advance into leadership? Or more strategically? The problem is that many of us buy into this belief that work equals results and that the harder we work the more results and success we will get. That if we just work hard enough it will speak for itself, that hard work pays off and it's all that's needed to succeed. That if we work hard enough, we will be enough.

Any Woman of Colour who has been successful in leadership and has had a seat at the proverbial table will tell you that yes it was difficult and yes, they had to work bloody hard but even though they have put in a load of hard work, their success was not determined solely by hard work. It alone was not sufficient to succeed as a Woman of Colour leader. Remember as discussed in earlier chapters, there are many people and Women of Colour in the world who have the capacity to work just as hard, if not harder than you; working longer hours, more intensively, getting more stuff done per hour than you. It's not about how hard you work, it's about what tasks you are choosing to get done; strategy. In my early 20s I started an online clothing store. I was working a full-time job and spent the rest of my waking hours on everything about my side hustle, except marketing and selling my clothes... I did job descriptions for jobs that didn't exist, invoice templates, set up systems, the whole thing but the one thing that mattered the most, that would determine success, was to get out from behind my brand and company and do the hard yards of selling and marketing my clothing. I didn't because I was too fearful and I let fear hold me back. It was so much easier to stay up till 5am in the morning creating systems and processes and ordering stock, rather than promote my company. This was when YouTube and Facebook were just taking off. Around that same time, Jane Lu also started an online clothing company and probably worked just as hard as me, but instead she chose to focus on marketing and selling and got onto Facebook, running campaigns and competitions. I continued to fiddle with my website and created systems for a company that only had sold a few items to some friends, had no outside investment or employees and didn't even need those systems, processes or policies. Today Jane's company, ShowPo, is reported to have a turnover of $85 million as of 2019 whereas I still have the clothes stock sitting in the wardrobe in my spare bedroom. Imagine if I had simply chosen to work hard at marketing like Jane instead of writing 20 job descriptions for my future, mega–successful clothing company that was non–existent at the time. Strategy equals results. Not hard work.

As a mentor and coach to driven and ambitious Women of Colour, I see this all the time.

> *Busyness has become the new addiction.*
>
> **#ColourFULL**

Much like food, we are obsessed with consumption as opposed to quality of nutrition. In our pursuit of goals, we look at doing as many tasks as possible rather than asking ourselves if they are the right tasks to occupy our focus and attention, or if the task we are about to do is the one that will take us closest towards achieving our goal and strategy in the shortest amount of time. It's like playing a game of darts, you want to take one dart and throw it smack bang on the middle of the target, not throw 10 and miss your target entirely; wasted time, energy and darts! The achievement of the desired result (hitting the red dot in the middle of the target) is in the skill and technique of throwing the dart (strategy) not in the quantity of darts being thrown or throwing itself (hard work). Be strategic. Hard work is not going to speak for itself. It's not going to go to your manager and say, 'Hey, Winitha has been working 10 hours, six days a week. Think she's up for a promotion?' Nope. Hard work is not going to do that for you, ever. Employers might hire you because their bias is that Women of Colour work hard (and can be paid less) or to hit a diversity quota but that bias doesn't get us into a leadership position. Hard work doesn't speak for itself, you do, so get visible and get talking. Get out from behind the desk and get in front of people. Let the right people (allies) know how hard you are working and importantly what you've done and achieved so they can leverage it to open doors of opportunity. Communicate it to them like a progress report and keep them consistently in the loop. Use communication strategies and messaging to let the right people know of your leadership goals, skills, experience, expertise and ability to get results. Hard work does not equal success and it is not enough to become and or be a leader. To thrive in White structures and become the leader you always knew you were, you need to focus on thinking strategically to work hard on the right tasks and draw visibility to you by communicating your personal brand, work ethic and outcomes to the right people (allies).

Shift your mindset from working harder to becoming more visible

In my conversations with Women of Colour, the one thing I keep hearing is a deep frustration about how working harder is not translating into progress. My invitation to you is to firstly understand where that belief stems from: is it about needing to prove or validate your self–worth; is it about trying to be heard seen and valued; is it a cultural belief or a belief that's a result of or caused by colonisation and systemic oppression? And lastly ask yourself, is this belief helpful or harmful and what is the impact of this belief to me?

A simple strategy to thrive in White structures is to shift your mindset and your focus from working hard, to being more visible. Deep down you know you have what it takes, you know you are a leader and are overly skilled and experienced for the job you have right now. You know that if you were given an opportunity that you would be so right for it and you would thrive. You don't need to work harder. Working hard is operational but being visible is strategic. Shift the tasks that get your attention and energy from operational to strategic. Visibility leads to being seen in front of the right people, the decision makers, movers and shakers who have the ability to provide you with opportunity. As Women of Colour, we are often not seen or heard and if we are not seen or heard how can we be considered for leadership positions and career growth opportunities? By resisting, pushing back, fighting against and revolting against the system we strategically seek ways to be visible because as mentioned above, hard work can't speak for itself and is not enough for us as Women of Colour to get noticed.

Visibility is key to activating and amplifying your personal brand.

#ColourFULL

A powerful personal brand is useless unless you get it in front of the right people; the people who need to see and experience your personal brand to then give you opportunities. Visibility opens doors and builds networks and relationships. After all, how can you build networks and relationships with key people who may have a leadership opportunity for you in the future if you are not visible? Visibility is the one thing that you can control in White structures. The idiots who see you rising and feel threatened, seeking to diminish your light or thwart your efforts, are evidence that you're rising in status and success towards your leadership goals. Your strategies and actions are working. So rather than being disappointed at idiots who might seek to sabotage your efforts, come back to your game plan, heal, reclaim your power, get support from a Woman of Colour mentor or coach, strategise, double down on your efforts, accelerate and stay two steps ahead of those idiots. You have all the skills and resources needed to navigate around and over them. These situations are a training ground to help you see and identify the red flags in the distance as they come up in the future; develop your own tools for staying visible despite what gets thrown your way; flex your anti-fragility muscle as well as strengthen your inner fitness game. The bigger the success and leadership responsibility, the greater the politics and challenges for Women of Colour. Don't let this stuff push you back, sharpen your senses and skills and stay on course.

One simple yet highly strategic way you can increase visibility is to join or put your hand up for organisational–wide projects. These are the projects that generally garner the most visibility internally and externally. These types of projects tend to give you exposure to departments and teams across the organisation as well as executive interaction giving you the opportunity to build networks and relationships and get in front of people who may have been previously hard to reach. In these positions, if there is an opportunity to present to a team, the organisation, CEO and or speak or be featured in the media, always be the first to grab those opportunities. The first task is to put your hand up and to get on the project. The second task is to ensure you are presenting as much as possible to amplify your visibility internally and externally. A second strategy is to use LinkedIn to find and speak at industry events and conferences. If you are struggling to be heard and valued in the organisation let alone to be seen/visible then seek opportunities outside the organisation. Remember, we must always stay in control of what we can control and let go what we can't and we can't control people. When organisations fail to give you a platform to be visible, let alone opportunities big or small, seek them externally with people who will. Put your hand up to speak and present at events, webinars, training programs and workshops. This all requires time so if you need to take a day or two off from work to prepare and to attend then take it. Losing a day's pay or giving up two days of annual leave will be worth it for a leadership job that will mostly likely come with a higher salary. As I said previously, 70% of jobs are in the hidden job market. It pays to be strategic.

Most of us have spent an awful lot of time on social media but I often wonder where all that investment of time and energy is getting you. I mean, is it helping you reach your goals? We need to spend our time strategically and master our social media skills on the platforms that will help us achieve our career and leadership goals. Your core audience is most likely not going to be on TikTok or Instagram unless you have a side hustle or are self–employed. Sure, there are people that have received opportunities on those platforms but if you are a team of one, already are working full–time with a myriad of other personal and professional commitments and want to climb up the corporate ladder, my advice is to use the little time you have on LinkedIn to get you in front of the right people. For those working in the community and social space this is the ideal place to be to network with other professionals that can support you in your leadership and social goals. Make sure your profile is completely filled out and strategically positioned for the next leadership job you want, not the job that you currently have or had five years ago. Build content that positions you as an expert and leader in your field and publish positive and value–adding content; content that offers something useful to those that have the decision–making power to give you that next opportunity or job. Content that solves a problem and outlines a solution.

Sorry, results don't speak for themselves either

Many fellow Thought Leaders that work in the gender equality space say that there is a myth around 'Build it and they will come' and I agree. There is a perception that if we do the work, apply for the job, interview well, get the project done, start the business that people will 'come' but this cannot be further from the truth. They say that it's not who you know, it's who you know that knows what about you that matters. For Women of Colour, it's not just who we know but that the right people and allies know the right information about us in order to take action to open doors, introduce you to contacts and networks, create opportunities and remove external barriers and challenges.

Get the evidence of your achievements and ability and make sure that you communicate it to the right people. One of the things I did in my past corporate career was to keep a secret file on my computer and put a monthly reminder in my calendar. Every month I would copy and paste any testimonials into my 'Successful Me' document and go through all my activities in my current role and document my results, quantitative (things that could be measured) and qualitative (things that couldn't be measured such as testimonials, stories, all the feel–good stuff). I went through any projects, did the maths and quantified them myself resulting in statements like 'Increased revenue by 70% in a three–month period.' Some of this information is easily accessible because you are capturing it as part of your tasks or reporting work but think outside the box and think broadly, there is a bunch of success and results you are achieving that can be quantified and captured but isn't because you are simply doing your job without that extra layer of tracking your own growth. In terms of qualitative information, simply brainstorm everything you have achieved in the past month, big and small. If you are struggling, go to your allies or trusted People of Colour colleagues and ask them what they thought you had done in the past month that made them think, 'Wow!' or 'Job well done.' Look at past emails for evidence, things your colleagues have commented on like, 'Thanks for the fast turnaround on this piece of work,' or 'X work is looking really great.' I also would write things people would say about me and my work in meetings or in and around the office in my notebook and highlight them for future reference.

The purpose of communicating the right results to the right people is to elevate and differentiate you from the rest. I bet no one else in your workplace is doing what you are doing.

As Women of Colour, we tend to hide behind our accomplishments thinking that if we have achieved something that it should be sufficient for us to advance and progress in our career.

#ColourFULL

But it's not. Just like hiding behind my online-store website didn't land me a $85 million company. We may also not view certain results as 'accomplishments' due to self-critical talk and internalised suppression, which is why it's important to check in with people we trust and respect. Importantly we need to celebrate all our achievements big and small. So, make it your business to let them know your business; what you are doing and achieving; what's in the pipeline; what you need support and help with; what you need them to do to propel you forward towards your leadership goals; how you are going and hell, even send them a party invite to celebrate your achievements! By doing this consistently you will elevate yourself and your success giving permission for sisters to also do the same.

Power dynamics

A third strategy to thriving in White structures is to understand the power dynamics of your environment. You cannot craft a strategy or game plan without first understanding the mechanics of White structures and systems. So, before you attempt to navigate and manage them let alone thrive in them, understand how they work at a deep level. Like any great battle, the offence must take time to understand the defence: the strengths, weaknesses, operational tactics, psychology and mindset; who all the key players are and how they work to anticipate what their moves might be on the battlefield and from there, strategies to overthrow and mitigate against them prior to battle.

The goal of offence is to anticipate the defences every move to train for and craft and execute a masterful game plan to ensure they win. For Women of Colour, it's no different. As discussed earlier in the book, create a power map and take the time to understand the organisation you work in, not just your department and breakdown and study all the power dynamics. These include where decisions are being made and the capacity of people and departments for certain decisions, big and small, as well as how one area influences another. Most organisations have hierarchical organisational structures that are easily accessible internally and sometimes people's job descriptions still exist on old job advertisements. Look to these for key responsibilities and, when you read between the lines, you can understand the decision–making power of those roles. By understanding the power dynamics that are at play you can then decide in advance the moves you can and need to make; the ones that are in your control in order to attain your leadership goals. Study your adversary intimately. View the organisation like a chessboard, a hierarchical, patriarchal, White, male and Western structure that operates like a machine. Intimately knowing how all the chess pieces move and the power differences and dynamics between them all will help you strategise your next leadership career move. As you step into leadership and become more visible you will be able to pinpoint where push might back come from and strategise proactively. It is not our job to dismantle and decolonise the system but if we desire to become the leader that we always knew we were, it is our job to understand the system intimately and deeply so that we can strategise to beat it at its own game.

In studying the power dynamics within an organisation, it can be helpful to educate yourself on commonly used terms in academia and research about systemic discrimination and racism and how these apply to power dynamics. You will have come across these words throughout this book: White feminism, fragility, tone–policing and so on. You can use these terms to understand more deeply the underlying, systemic roots of internal and external barriers. Understanding the root and how the system operates empowers and equips us to effectively reclaim our power, heal and strategise. It also enables us to craft an effective leadership game plan and flex our inner fitness to masterfully execute on this plan. It gives us the strategies, tools, skills, language and support structure to navigate and manage White structures so that individually and collectively we thrive. Understanding these terms can give us comfort and healing in knowing that our individual experiences are often shared experiences for other Women and People of Colour and are real and true. This will also give us language that helps articulate our own unique experiences and circumstances to ourselves and others. A word of caution, I advise that you engage in healing and self-care prior to studying up on these terms. Reading and studying the below content can be retraumatising and distressing for some. I recommend creating a study group with other Women of Colour who are also already engaged in self-healing and self-care so that you have a safe space and community support to do the work needed to propel you into leadership and success; sisterhood, soul soothing, heart uplifting. If you aren't familiar with some of these terms your homework is to research and study up on them:

White saviour

Centring

White feminism

White fragility, tears

White silencing, politeness

\# Tone–policing

\# Sexism and feminism

\# Racism (critical race theory, individual, interpersonal, structural, institutionalised, colonisation)

\# Ancestral history (talk with your grandparents, aunties and uncles)

\# White privilege and supremacy

\# Spiritual bypassing

\# Cultural appropriation and misappropriation

\# Bias (conscious/unconscious/implicit), micro and macro aggressions

\# Systemic discrimination and racism

\# Intersectionality

\# Cultural and psychological safety

\# The office 'housework'

\# Internalised suppression

\# Intergenerational and ancestral trauma

\#   Repression, Oppression and suppression

\#   Political constructs

So, dear Sister, here we are at the end of this book. My desire, goal, dream and my blessing to you is that by activating the strategies, tools and tactics from the entire book you will succeed into leadership. As a Woman of Colour leader myself, I know that you have what it takes and more to become who you always knew you were: a powerful leader that transforms the world. Know that whatever room you go into, whatever meeting you sit in, whatever person you talk to, I am there with you in spirit and so too are your ancestors and sisters. You won't fall, we're standing behind you, we'll catch you. We're walking and taking every step with you in this incredible journey. Mark my words, it will be absolutely worth it. You are worth the effort. The journey is worth it. You have what it takes and more. You are deserving of this dream.

Now that you have read this book, it's time to create and craft a brilliant strategy with all the tools you have learned here and train for it like you were going into battle; work on your psychological, spiritual, emotional, intellectual and physical fitness and learn to execute like a pro. You will thrive and you will succeed. There may be only a few Women of Colour who have succeeded into leadership but therein lies the blueprint. The blueprint is in this book. If they can and if I can then you can.

\#   *You are our future. The world needs us and our leadership.*

#ColourFULL

Know that knowledge is not power, it's the application and execution of knowledge that is power. The answers in this book have worked for the hundreds of Women of Colour I train, mentor and coach on a daily basis through my leadership and business programs, events and initiatives. I have seen Women of Colour achieve more in six months through working with me than they have on their own in the past two to five years. If they can, you can too. All it takes is a little expert support (me), structure (this book) and accountability (your sisters). You have the power, the skills and the courage to stand up, resist, push back, fight back, against the system and beat it as its own game individually and even more powerfully as a collective, a sisterhood. Build anti—fragility and then build it some more, this is your armour. Your weaponry, game plan, training and tools are in this book. So, train and strategise, train and strategise and then do it all over again.

You're ready to step into leadership and take action now and I just know that your life is going to change in such a significant way with breakthrough after breakthrough. Your ancestors and the sisterhood have got your back. Let's do this together. I believe in you, dear Sister. Go claim that which is rightfully yours for yourself, your culture, your community, your sisters and generations to come. Freedom awaits you on the other side. Revolt and begin your revolution. It starts today. BE the revolution and be blest.

Gratefully yours in service and sisterhood,

Winitha Bonney

xo

Share the quotes in this chapter with others
so that they too can be elevated, empowered and inspired.

Remember to tag Winitha so that we can reshare
your post with our global community.
Turn to p274 for Winitha's social media handles.

Connect with me

#ColourFULL conference

#ColourFULL is a leadership and entrepreneurship conference by and for Women of Colour and allies. At this vibrant, energetic and empowering conference you will find a supportive and positive community and learn tools and strategies to thrive in your career, business and life. You will also meet clever, ambitious and driven Women of Colour just like you, have the opportunity to be mentored and find a mentor as well as meet and hear from exceptional Women of Colour leaders who will enable you to 'see it to be it' as well as unpack the steps they took to get a seat at the table. Think of #ColourFULL as a TED talk crossed with a Beyonce concert! To find out more head to www.winitha.com/colourfull

Women of Colour private community

Join a private community by and for Women of Colour only. In this community you will be empowered, elevated and educated to succeed in your career, business and life through online forums and community conversations, content, courses, workshops, virtual events, training programs, coaching, community and mentoring. To find out more head to www.winitha.com

Leadership and business programs and workshops

Winitha offers a range of one–on–one and group–based leadership and business training, coaching and mentoring programs as well as online self–paced programs that are nuanced and tailored to the unique needs of Women and People of Colour. She also runs monthly live webinars and workshops on topics from ancestral healing to high performance leadership and thriving in white structures. To find out more head to www.winitha.com

Socials

Instagram @winitha.bonney

Facebook www.facebook.com/winithabonney/

LinkedIn Winitha Bonney

Biography

*"You wanna fly...you got to give up the sh*t that weighs you down."*

~ Toni Morrison

Winitha Bonney is one of the world's foremost thinkers in leadership and entrepreneurship for Women and People of Colour and a global expert in helping organisations build inclusive cultures and communities. She has over two decades of experience in executive roles, has founded several businesses and embraces her multiple lived experiences. This has provided Winitha with the unique insight and expertise to support Women of Colour to become leaders and successful entrepreneurs and create inclusive equitable working cultures for Women of Colour.

She has run leadership events, workshops and programs in corporate and government organisations and mentored over 200 Women of Colour one-on-one. Women of Colour from around the world have written to Winitha to tell her the courage they have gained from engaging with her and how she has supported their healing, growth, success and abundance. Winitha's strength is breaking down success stories and complex strategies into steps to take Women of Colour through 'how she did that' to see that 'if she could, I can too.'

Winitha is the founder of #ColourFULL, a leadership and entrepreneurship conference and awards night by Women of Colour for Women of Colour and allies. She also runs a digital platform and growing private membership community of over 800 Women of Colour where she empowers, elevates and educates them to succeed in their career, business and life through online content, courses, workshops, virtual events, training programs, coaching, community and mentoring. Her programs and online community provide you with a safe environment, support, accountability, training and the mentorship you need to achieve your desired outcomes.

She also works with corporate and government organisations to equip and empower the People and Women of Colour in their organisation to become powerful leaders that transform the world through coaching and mentoring programs and leadership training.

In 2021, she was awarded an Order of Australia Medal for her extensive work in diversity and inclusion and in the community. Winitha holds a Masters of Arts (Management), Masters of Marketing, Bachelor of Business (Distinction) and an Advanced Diploma in International Trade, is a qualified and trained leadership and business coach and has extensive professional development certifications in business, leadership and innovation.

Think of Winitha as a personal trainer for your career and business goals. If you are struggling, you don't have to do it alone. If you're stuck, you don't have to stay stuck. Send a private message to www.winitha.com and we will get you the help you need and deserve.

Why I wrote this book

Around May 2019 I started getting the 'call' to write this book. God started pulling and tugging at my heart every day. In June the call became unbearingly loud and emotionally and physically excruciating. I tried ignoring it but it only kept getting louder and louder. Writing this book also didn't feel like the commercial thing to do for my practice or therefore the priority. I also know that self–publishing is not cheap (think 5 figures!) and rarely do you recoup the funds through book sales. Could I let go of my precious savings for a book that might not have any impact for my sisters? These were my fears. However, I knew from previous life experience to not ignore the tug of your heart when God comes knocking on your door with a purpose and a calling! In July I gave in. I declared, 'God! You win!' I cleared my diary and in less than two and a half weeks over 105 000 words easily poured out of me like water. This was the confirmation that I needed. A few days later after completing the book I had a powerful spiritual experience; a vision of the #ColourFULL conference. Me on stage looking out to a sea of more than 600 beautiful gorgeous, talented and gifted Black, Brown, First Nations and Women of Colour faces. You and I were dancing the same dance, to the same song, singing the same words, having the time of our lives. Among the laughter, singing and dancing I could feel the immense weight and burden of the pain and sadness you had been hiding and carrying for years. Your souls were suffering and slowly drowning. And in that moment tears poured and streamed out of my brown eyes with my heart screaming out to yours saying.... 'If only you knew...'

www.ingramcontent.com/pod-product-compliance
Lightning Source LLC
Chambersburg PA
CBHW062118020426
42335CB00013B/1011